THE CRICKETS ALL LOOK ALIKE

Books by Bill Davidson:

THE CRICKETS ALL LOOK ALIKE

SIX BRAVE PRESIDENTS

THE REAL AND THE UNREAL

The Crickets
All Look Alike

by Bill Davidson

ILLUSTRATED BY BOB BUGG

HARPER & ROW, PUBLISHERS / NEW YORK

ONCE AGAIN TO MURIEL—BUT ALSO TO
CAROL AND HER NEW YOUNG HUSBAND, HAP

THE CRICKETS ALL LOOK ALIKE

chapter 1

O ne day in 1960, my wife, Muriel, an asp-tongued
    redhead, was poking around in a Connecticut
antique shop and she found an old beat-up sign that
read: THE BRAEBURN INN. The sign had once hung outside a Colonial inn in Sherman, Connecticut, and the
gilt paint was all flaked and it looked pretty ratty and
the frame was scorched from when the inn had burned
down about fifty years ago. But Muriel bought the sign
for fifteen dollars and she brought it home to our
sparkling-new contemporary apartment in New York
City and she looked at the sign reflectively and she
said, "We've got to buy a house to go with it."

That's how it all began.

We decided to hold a family meeting to discuss the
proposal. The participants in the meeting were myself,
as chairman, Muriel, and our daughter, Carol, an asp-

tongued brunette, who was then seventeen years old and a freshman in college. Also present, in a non-voting capacity, was our Panamanian housekeeper, Naomi. Naomi's contribution to the meeting was a suggestion that we get a cow and some chickens to go along with the house which we were considering buying to go along with the sign. "I will take care of the cow and the chickens," Naomi announced, "and then when you go broke at least you will have milk to drink and *arroz con pollo* to eat." This motion on the floor received considerable support from Carol and caused some uneasiness among the other two members, but it was voted down.

This matter having been disposed of, we next turned to finances. I had just previously received a small windfall from one of my books and Muriel was piling up a little money from her magazine articles and television appearances. This disclosure by Muriel, the finance committee, caused me momentary pleasure though I scowled at Carol upon the realization that *she* as yet was not bringing a cent into the house. We discussed our unaccustomed surplus in the bank and Muriel said, "Who needs stocks and bonds anyway, with the economy of the country the way it is." I assented agreeably (it didn't occur to me until later that I had never *considered* buying stocks and bonds, and the economy of the country had never been more sound). "OK," I said, "that takes care of the money for the down payment. Now where should we buy this house to go along with the sign?"

Muriel said, "There's only one place—Connecticut. It

should be a house that goes back at least to the Revolutionary War." She added sternly and with questionable logic, "You know your father was born in Latvia and my people came from Wales and we need *roots* in American history. Maybe we could even find a place on a Revolutionary War battlefield and dig up cannonballs in the back yard." Carol said, "Good. I always loved the story of Pickett's Charge." I said, scowling again, "That was the *Civil* War, dear, which took place several hundred miles to the south of Connecticut. Give me the names of your history teachers in high school. I must write to them about the way they educated you." The following Sunday we went house-hunting in Connecticut.

We started in Ridgefield, for no other reason than our dentist lived there, and that seemed as good a way to start as any. The first house we looked at was on a lake, directly next door to the dentist. In fact, it was only about ten feet from the dentist's home. The dentist had recommended it. Muriel's nesting instincts had already taken over and she was poking happily about in the basement, for some reason known only to her, when I said, "Dear, don't you think this house is a little close to the dentist's?" Muriel said, "But that's an *advantage*. You know how you sometimes get those toothaches in the middle of the night." I switched to another tack and said, "But how about the Revolutionary War? I doubt if this house goes back to Harry Truman. How would your Revolutionary War sign look on a Korean War house?" The nesting instinct visibly evaporated and she said, "You're right." We thereupon decided jointly that it might be better to go to a real estate agent to look for a house instead of to a dentist.

We found a real estate agent through a friend and on subsequent weekends we invaded western Connecticut looking for a proper place to hang the sign. We came upon a converted Colonial barn deep in the woods near the village of New Fairfield and our enthusiasm mounted. I was about to ask for the papers to sign, when the real estate agent, a handsome and taciturn young man named Jay Morrow, dourly asked, "Are you folks planning to live here in the winter?" "Why, sure," we replied. "Don't know how you're going to make it," he observed. "Half mile from the road, two, three feet of snow. Maybe snowshoes?" "Let's get out of here," I said.

The next gem we discovered was another converted barn in the town of Bridgewater, overlooking some forty acres of magnificent Berkshire Mountain landscape. For some reason, the sight of the house caused Carol to weep. "This is the house I've always wanted to live in," she sniffed. "I've seen it in my dreams for years." "How much?" I asked Morrow. "Cheap," he said, "but—" By now experienced with Morrow's "buts," I did not stay for an answer but made a closer personal examination of the premises. There were certain deficiencies in the reconstruction of the barn which Muriel and I noted almost simultaneously. "What's *that?*" shrieked Muriel, and she pointed to a toilet, sink and tub standing in unwalled majesty in the middle of the floor. Morrow didn't answer directly. "House is twenty thousand," he said. "Cost you maybe another twenty to fix it up. The owner ran out of money and never finished." "Let's get out of here," I said. Carol wept all the way back to New York.

During the ride, Muriel became morose and quiet. I ignored this condition since she and Carol frequently have sympathetic reactions, causing their moods to coincide nicely. As we entered the city limits of New York, Muriel spoke for the first time in thirty miles. "Maybe we ought to forget this whole idea," she said. "Do we want to be like those suburbanites and ex-urbanites and live in a town with all that drinking and wife-swapping?"

"Any town like that can't be all bad," I observed.

This was, I discovered, the wrong thing to say.

Two weeks later, when the wounds caused by my remark had healed, we went house-hunting anew. This time the imperturbable Jay Morrow took us into the rural countryside near Danbury (we knew it was rural because there were lots of black-and-white cows chewing their cuds in fields alongside the road) and he showed us a house we all hated on sight. Morrow said, "You want a genuine Colonial? This is a genuine Colonial. Built around 1740. They call it the John Wilkes house. John Wilkes Booth—you know, the feller shot Lincoln—lived here as a boy. Guess John Wilkes was his uncle or something." The house was red clapboard and it looked authentic enough to me because I had once seen a reconstructed Colonial village in Sturbridge, Massachusetts, and all those houses looked like this house. But it seemed stark to me, and Carol said, "Look at those little windows. They look like portholes," and Muriel said, "My, but it's close to the road." Morrow commented dryly, "That's the way Colonial folks lived."

We went inside and met the owners, a couple named Ruth and Joe Bates, who had two small sons, one of whom looked exactly like Alfred E. Neuman on the cover of *Mad* magazine. We warmed up slightly to the charm of the interior of the house, but Muriel said, "Everything's so *small*," and I uttered my usual exit line, "Let's get out of here." We went away and looked at other houses, but later in the afternoon Muriel inexplicably said to Morrow, "Let's go back and see the Bates place again." We did, with the same result. Muriel said, "Everything *still* looks so small."

We were drawn back to the Bates house again on two succeeding Sundays. After our fourth visit, Muriel grew thoughtful in the car and I knew something was in the making. I held my peace and finally Muriel said, "How tall do you think Joe Bates is?" I said, "Oh, about six-six, six-seven." She said, "And about how tall do you think Ruth Bates is?" I said, "She's a pretty big lady, maybe six-two." "That's *it*," Muriel exclaimed in triumph. "*What's* it?" I said, narrowly missing a truckload of apples pulling out of an orchard. She said, "They're so *big* and that's what makes the house look so *small*. They even have big furniture so they can fit into it. Joe

Bates told me himself that he likes a long couch that he can stretch out on and I bet that's why you can't open the front door."

I assented vaguely. Muriel said, "Now let's go back there and imagine that everything, including the Bateses, are normal-sized and let's see what happens." It sounded like an interesting exercise in higher mathematics to me, if nothing else, so we went back. While the Bateses looked on in puzzlement, we imagined Joe to be five feet eleven inches and Ruth to be five feet eight inches, and their sons to be three feet tall instead of four feet, and the couch to be five feet long instead of eight feet. My own concentration was interrupted when I saw Joe crack his head on the doorframe between the kitchen and the living room, but on the whole, the imagining went rather well. I hustled Muriel out of the house and into the car. She was bubbling. I said, "But how about the windows like portholes and being so close to the road?" "That," she said indignantly, "is how Colonial folks lived."

We drove in silence for about ten miles and then suddenly Muriel shouted, "Stop!" I thought I had run a red light, but seeing nothing but maple trees in the vicinity, I said, "Why?" Muriel said, "Now I *know* we ought to buy the Bates house." I pulled the car over to await the explanation I knew was coming and which I knew would have something to do with the philosophy of Muriel's late Welsh grandmother, whom she always quotes in moments of great decision. Muriel said, "I left my purse in the Bates house and my Welsh grandmother always told me that when you leave your purse somewhere, that place really belongs to you." So we turned around and got Jay Morrow out of bed and signed an agreement that night to buy the Bates house.

Several interminable weeks later, Muriel and I were summoned to a ritual called "a closing" at the New Milford Savings Bank in New Milford, Connecticut. We left Carol in the car, entered the bank and were ushered into a conference room, where we were seated on one side of a large table with the Bateses placed on the other side, as if we were antagonists of some sort. A man from the bank was there along with the bank's lawyer, a friendly, red-faced man whom everyone called Attorney Anderson, never "Mister" and never by his first name. "It must be some sort of Connecticut custom, like calling a doctor 'Doctor,' " Muriel whispered. Attorney Anderson, to open the meeting, passed out fly swatters with the name of the bank on them and Muriel again whispered, "This must be part of the closing ritual up here in Connecticut." We all sat silently for a while, swatting flies, as we waited for my attorney to arrive from New York.

My attorney, a tall, earnest man named Irwin Taylor who teaches at Brooklyn Law School and who was more at home handling copyright matters, got there about ten minutes late. He and Attorney Anderson eyed each other suspiciously. Then Attorney Anderson riffled his papers like a country poker expert about to deal a nondescript hand to a city slicker, and the ritual began. The lawyers argued back and forth in their unintelligible language while we and the Bateses smiled at each other embarrassedly and swatted more flies. Occasionally Attorney Anderson would look up and say something neighborly to try to put us at our ease. At one point he said, "Nice piece of property you're buying there. Know it well. Beautiful view of the lake." And he returned to his poker game with Taylor.

Muriel looked at me with eyes wider than usual. "Did he say *lake?*" she hissed in my ear. I got the message and broke in on Attorney Anderson. "*What* lake, sir?" I asked. "*What* lake?" repeated Attorney Anderson with amusement. "Don't you know you're going to live on Candlewood, the largest and most beautiful body of water in this part of the country?" By this time the Bateses were looking at him with bewilderment, too, and something seemed to dawn on Attorney Anderson. His red face grew redder. He said, "Aren't you Joseph Bates of Barnum Road in New Fairfield?" "No," said Joe, "I'm Joseph Bates of Route 37A in Danbury." Attorney Anderson buried his head in his hands and then stared at the man from the bank. "Oh, my God," he said, "we searched the title on the wrong house." The drama of the situation intrigued me and I asked brightly, "What would have happened if I signed these papers? Would the other Joe Bates have to give me this house?" Both attorneys ignored me.

By now Attorney Anderson was acting like a poker player who had dealt himself a four flush. The tide of battle had turned and Taylor, with a smug look on his face, was in complete charge of the situation. He suggested something called "escrow," and Attorney Anderson accepted. I asked Taylor, "Is escrow good or bad?" Impatient even in victory, Taylor said, "It's OK. Just you and Muriel sign here." We signed. The rest of the closing was quite boring since we ran out of flies to swat as the lawyers argued. Toward the very end, however, we were amused to see Attorney Anderson pick up the final winning hand in the poker game. Taylor said triumphantly, "Just one more thing. You've made *another* mistake. It says here the taxes are only ninety-six dollars for these three acres and the eight-room house. You've misplaced the decimal point. I'm sure it should be nine hundred and sixty dollars." All the joy that had drained from Attorney Anderson's face returned. "Where *you* come from, Mr. Taylor," he exclaimed, "the taxes undoubtedly would be nine hundred and sixty dollars. But up here we pride ourselves in prudent, low-cost, uncorrupted local government. The taxes, I can assure you, are ninety-six dollars." Taylor slunk away to catch his train back to New York.

The rest of us concluded the closing with a few pleasantries and as we shook hands all around, the Bateses said, "We're pretty much moved out of the house. You can go right over there now, if you want to." Muriel, Carol and I sped the ten miles from New Milford to our new domicile. It looked beautiful and even large, with the giant Bateses no longer in residence. We wandered from room to room, making decoration plans.

Carol struck off on her own. Suddenly we heard her excited voice coming from one of the bedrooms. She shrieked, "Our *beds* are here. Bloomingdale's delivered them already." We rushed into the bedroom and there, indeed, were neatly cartoned box springs and mattresses. Carol said, "We don't have bed clothes, but maybe we can sleep here tonight anyway?" She pleaded, *"Can* we?"

I looked at Muriel, got the signal and said, "OK." We then fell to, exuberantly ripping the mattress cartons apart. Abruptly, however, Muriel said, "Wait a minute. We didn't buy *used* mattresses, did we?" "Of course not," I replied. "Well," said Muriel with a sense of foreboding, "these mattresses are used and they're very big." "Oh, oh," I said, "let's get out of here." "Oh, no you don't," said Muriel. "You'll have to find a hardware store and buy masking tape and patch the Bateses' mattress cartons back together again."

The repair job took about an hour. Then, disconsolately, we made ready to go back to New York. On the way out, Muriel said, "Wait a minute. There's still one thing we have to do." She rushed out to the car and came struggling back with her battered Braeburn Inn sign, which she had secreted in the trunk. She announced proudly, "We're not going to be suburbanites, we're not going to be exurbanites. We're going to be in a class by ourselves—Braeburnites. Put it up."

I took the sign from her and moved to the front of the house, where I knew there were some hooks on which it could hang. Muriel yelled, "Where are you

going?" I said, "I am going to the front of the house to hang up the sign." Muriel said, "Are you out of your mind? Do you want total strangers to come in here looking for food and drink. It will be bad enough with your family."

"Well, where *else* would you hang an inn sign?" I asked.

"On the *back* of the house, of course, where nobody can see it," said Muriel.

Without questioning her reasoning, I hung the sign on the back of the house—and our great adventure as Braeburnites had begun.

chapter ii

We got to sleep in our house about a week later.
The beds had now arrived, but nothing else.
There really was no reason to move into the house yet,
but we wanted to examine it at our leisure without the
Bateses around to watch us suspiciously, and Carol had
an uncontrollable yen to sleep in the little room upstairs where she was sure John Wilkes Booth, at the age
of about sixteen, had plotted the assassination of President Lincoln. I thought of explaining to her that when
John Wilkes Booth lived in the house, Abraham Lincoln was still practicing law in Springfield, Illinois, and
no one this side of the Appalachian Mountains had ever
heard of him, but I held my tongue so as not to dampen
her adolescent enthusiasms.

Muriel and I, being more complex both by nature
and by reason of age, tempered our own enthusiasms

with considerable trepidation. Neither of us had ever lived in the country before. I had been born and raised in Jersey City, New Jersey, and my only exposure to nature had been in two-week summer hitches in boys' camps. Usually it had rained during most of the two weeks, however, and I had devoted myself to winning bicycle money playing poker with the other kids in the bunkhouse. In my twenty-year career as a magazine writer, nearly all of my time had been spent in the big cities of the world, except when I had covered wars; and country living in wars is, to say the least, atypical.

Muriel, too, was a big-city girl—from St. Paul, Minnesota—and the only rural-experience advantage she had on me was the fishing trips in northern Wisconsin on which she had gone with her father. From Minnesota, after she graduated from college, she had migrated to Hollywood, where she became a movie press agent and, later, being young and attractive, a TV panelist. Now she also was the second magazine-writer member of our little family. Rural living to *her*, theretofore, had meant camping out in a luxury motel for a few weeks during the shooting of a western movie on location in Colorado or Arizona.

When we drove up to our newly acquired house for the first time, these thoughts weighed heavily on us— but only until the prim old red-painted structure loomed up with majestic dignity as we drove around the last bend in the road and saw it through the lush green trees. Then all our bubbling excitement returned.

We arrived early in the afternoon, laden with toilet

paper and other necessities, and Carol, overwhelmed with her sense of history, insisted that we drop everything and go immediately for a walk in the woods, which cover about two-thirds of our property, to look for Revolutionary cannonballs. We climbed a steep path into the woods (the house is just below the summit of 1,100-foot Titicus Mountain, the highest point of land in the area) and after battling our way through thicket and bramble for a few minutes, we climbed a stone fence and came upon an old abandoned dirt road. Muriel squealed with joy. "This must be that old road Jay Morrow told us about"—she beamed—"the one the minutemen built to attack the British from the rear when they occupied Danbury."

She and Carol ran happily up the weed-choked lane, peering into the moss-covered stone walls which lined it, looking, I presumed, for rusted muskets. Suddenly, about fifty feet ahead, Muriel yelled, "Look at that old sign! I bet the minutemen put it up to mark an ammunition dump or something." She rushed over to the sign, which indeed was very old and curled around the edges and was tacked with rusty antique nails to a tree. Before I could reach her, she and Carol had fallen back from the tree in red-faced disarray. "Don't bother to look at the sign," she said sternly. "It's nothing." Naturally, I then walked over to look at the Revolutionary relic. In neat hand lettering the sign said, "S——t to you." By the time I had stopped laughing, Muriel and Carol had walked primly a quarter of a mile up the road.

We followed the old road to the top of the mountain

and down the far slope—a distance of about four miles —without encountering any other *graffiti*, antique or otherwise. There were no people or signs of human habitation, either. Just the omnipresent stone fences stretching off every hundred feet or so into the dense forest. Occasionally there was a plowed field planted in hay or corn in one of the rectangles formed by the stone fences. In the old road we could see tire tracks leading off into the planted fields, which explained why the road itself hadn't long since been overgrown by the forest; it was obviously used by farmers to get to these remote fields for seeding and harvesting, and their tractors periodically knocked down the saplings and the underbrush. Carol was disappointed. "What kind of Colonial atmosphere is *this?*" she lamented. Muriel pointed to the old stone walls. "Who do you think put *those* up?" she said sagely. "The Connecticut Highway Department?" asked Carol. "No," said Muriel in exasperation, "the Colonial farmers built those walls to divide their fields when they cleared the land two hundred fifty years ago." "How did you know *that?*" I asked. "*You* told me," said Muriel. "Oh," I said. Listening to this exchange, Carol remained totally unconvinced.

When we got home and commenced to explore the house at our leisure, it was a different matter. Carol went down to the basement and squealed, "I found something!" We rushed down the rickety wooden steps and there was what seemed to be a roughhewn fireplace in the cellar. "What's a fireplace doing in the cellar, O fount of all knowledge?" Muriel asked me. To preserve my family reputation, I mumbled something about having to go to the bathroom, rushed upstairs and made a surreptitious phone call to Jay Morrow. "What's a fireplace doing in the basement?" I whispered. "That's not a fireplace," he whispered back, "that's a smoke oven where the Colonial folks used to cure their hams." I hastened down to the cellar and announced, "I just figured out what that fireplace is. It isn't a fireplace at all. It's a smoke oven where the Colonial folks used to cure their hams." Muriel looked at me suspiciously, but she reexamined the blackened ancient stones and assented. "What'll we use it for?" Carol inquired. "To shrink heads, dear," said Muriel. "It'll save your father's friends a lot of psychiatrist bills."

Upstairs we found other satisfactory signs of great age. The big fieldstone fireplace in the living room obviously had been there for years, and throughout the house the rough-cut exposed oaken beams were pegged together, not nailed, and when I tapped one with a hammer it was so petrified with age that it gave out a ringing, stonelike sound. The floors, no longer covered by the Bateses' carpeting, were wide, irregular planks. On one door Carol found a hand-forged hook, obviously made by a blacksmith, the point of which, swinging back and forth for more than two centuries, had worn away a semicircular groove in the planks of the door. In the kitchen there were a General Electric stove on high bowed legs and an equally elderly washing machine. They were not exactly Colonial, but as we were to find out the moment we attempted to use them, they *did* qualify as antiques. We later discovered that every wily Yankee householder keeps a set of such ancient appliances in the basement against the day when he sells his house. His new appliances move out with him; the relics come up from the basement to fill the gaps in the kitchen for the new owner.

By the time Muriel had recovered from the shock of this revelation, she had eked out a dinner of hamburgers and frozen potatoes for us (Naomi, our housekeeper, had wisely elected to remain behind in the New York apartment) and we were ready to go to bed. Carol retired to John Wilkes Booth's plotting room, where she listened to the creaking beams and reported happily every few minutes, until she fell into her untroubled seventeen-year-old's sleep, that Booth's ghost was walking about and casing the new inhabitants. "I think that's squirrels, dear," said Muriel after the tenth report, but Carol didn't hear her.

Muriel and I read for a while, sitting on the floor of the living room with our backs propped against suit cases, and finally we hit the sack in the downstairs master bedroom. I was just in that delicious stage between sleep and wakefulness when Muriel nudged me. "I can't stand it," she said. "You can't stand *what?*" I asked. "The noise," she said. I sat up and listened, but compared with the traffic sounds which accompanied all our sleeping hours in the New York apartment, it was like the inside of a library. "Have you been drinking?" I asked Muriel. "Of *course* not," she said with considerable indignation. "Don't you hear them?"

"Hear *who?*" I almost screamed.

"The crickets, you idiot," she said. "They're hollering their little heads off."

"Crickets don't holler," I said. "They rub their little legs together."

"*You* must have been drinking," she said.

"No, I really mean it," I said. "They make that noise by rubbing their legs together."

"Oh, so you *do* hear the noise," she said. "Then why don't you go out and do something about it?"

"OK, so I hear the crickets," I said, "but what do you expect me to do?"

"We have a can of insect spray in the kitchen. Why don't you go out and kill them?"

"For the same reason, my darling, that I can't go out and kill the whole Chinese Army. If I kill one cricket, another cricket will just move in and take its place."

"But there's one big cricket that's hollering louder than the others. If you could just kill *him* . . ."

"He's not hollering, dear, he's rubbing his little legs together. Besides, the crickets all look alike. But I'll try."

I struggled out of bed, got the can of insect spray and went outside. I sat on a rock and smoked a cigarette and then went back and told Muriel I had killed the big cricket. "But I still hear him," she said.

"Just like the Chinese Army," I said smugly. "They brought up a replacement already."

Muriel sulked for a while and I smoked another cigarette. Finally I said, "Tell you what I'm gonna do. You don't hear the traffic noise in New York because we've got air conditioners, right?"

"Right," she said.

"OK," I said, "I'll buy you an air conditioner to drown out the crickets."

She said, "Where can you find a store that will sell you an air conditioner at two o'clock in the morning?"

"Nowhere," I said, "but in the meantime I'll get that fan I saw in the window in the attic and put it in our window and you won't hear the crickets any more."

"Good thinking," Muriel said.

I climbed the stairs to the attic and Carol heard me and screamed, thinking it really *was* John Wilkes Booth's ghost. I calmed her by saying, "It's only me, trying to drown out some crickets." "Oh," Carol said, being accustomed to such dialogue in our house, and she went back to sleep.

I unscrewed the fan from the attic window and struggled downstairs with it. I left both the fan and the screwdriver in the kitchen, in the firm belief—based on long experience—that Muriel would by now be sound asleep. She was, and I dragged my weary body into the bed. But now *I* couldn't sleep. The one big cricket seemed to have moved directly under the window and he really *was* hollering his head off. At 4 A.M., with Muriel snoring peacefully away, I finally got up, brought the fan from the kitchen into the bedroom and set it in the window. I turned it on and with the steady drone to remind me of New York, I drifted off, at last, into troubled dreams.

chapter iii

The next morning, Muriel, being merciful by nature, let me sleep until eight o'clock and when I finally lurched out into the living room, I found her staring at a candy box. "That's funny," she said, "I could swear I left jelly beans in this box and now there's nothing but these little pellets of chocolate. I don't remember having any candy like that." She moved her hand to the box in an automatic reaction to taste the pellets. Some warning light went on in my sleep-befuddled brain, probably a flashback to my Boy Scout days, and I bellowed, "Don't!"

"Why not?" Muriel asked.

"Because," I said, "I don't think that is chocolate. I think that is mouse droppings. I think field mice came in during the night and ate the jelly beans and those little pellets is what mice do after they eat."

There was a delayed scream from both Muriel and Carol and they both flung themselves out of the house. When I caught up with them they were sitting stonily in the car. "Take me back to New York," Muriel demanded. It took me a half hour to convince the two females who looked to me for leadership that the field mice would not come into the house during the daylight hours while we were there, and that by nightfall I would have engaged the services of an exterminator. They finally acceded and came back into the house, but only on the condition that I would remove the candy box and bury it in the woods.

That's the kind of day it started out to be.

Our next disaster befell us soon after. When we had bought the house, we were delighted with the wallpaper and other decoration except in one place—our bedroom. Whereas the rest of the house had been done in tasteful Colonial design, the master bedroom had a sickly, dark-green, circled wallpaper, but Muriel, who had been studying and absorbing television commercials, said the circles had to go. "I saw a wonderful new paint on TV," she said. "It doesn't drip and you can wash your brushes in water and it covers right over wallpaper. There was a girl in the commercial wearing an evening dress and she painted a whole room and was ready to serve a formal dinner without changing her clothes." So we had arrived with two gallons of the wondrous paint. A bright yellow.

At about 11 A.M., after Muriel and Carol had recovered from the trauma of the mouse turds, we settled down to painting the bedroom. Muriel didn't have an evening gown with her, so she wore tailored slacks and a silk blouse. I wore my usual working costume (while writing or otherwise) of tattered T-shirt, chino pants and bare feet. Carol wore shorts and a black sweatshirt she had picked up somewhere, which bore the legend, in white, across the chest, "Alcoholics Anonymous." In about twenty minutes, we all seemed to be dressed the same—in speckled yellow. We also had speckled yellow hair, speckled yellow faces, and I had speckled yellow insteps.

The yellow seemed to be going everywhere but on the walls. We rolled it on the green wallpaper with rollers and we sloshed it on the green wallpaper with brushes, but still the ugly green circles stared through at us like a thousand evil little eyes. Then Muriel said, "My God, look at that!" We turned to the section she had been working on and the wallpaper was ballooning from the wall in a huge five-foot-high bubble. Carol said, "My God, look at *that!*" We turned to the section *she* was working on and the wallpaper was separating from the wall in strips, wherever sections of it had come together. We put down our brushes and rollers and just stared dumbly as we watched the wallpaper ballooning and separating everywhere.

"Well, what do we do now?" Muriel said.

I said, "As I remember the commercial, we're now supposed to rinse off our rollers and brushes in water and serve a formal dinner, dressed as we are."

"Very funny," said Muriel.

We all trooped disconsolately into the kitchen, deposited our paint-laden implements in the sink and I turned on the water.

There was no water.

"Turn the faucet," said Muriel.

"I *have* turned the faucet. Nothing's happening."

I rushed to the two bathrooms, turned the taps and flushed the toilets.

"No water," I murmured.

"Well, *do* something!" shrieked Muriel. "Call the Water Department."

I explained, "There *is* no Water Department way out here in the country. There are no water mains. Our water belongs to us. Somewhere on this property there is a well, and somewhere there is a pump, and the pump pulls the water out of the ground and it runs out of our faucets, see?"

"No," said Muriel. "Go call the Water Department."

"If you insist," I said, and I phoned the Water Department of the City of Danbury. I explained my plight to a rather amused man and he said, "Are you kidding? Our nearest water main is about five miles from your house. No, look, Mac, somewhere on your property there is a well, and somewhere there is a pump, and—"

"Never mind," I said, "I know." I was too stricken inside even to smirk triumphantly at Muriel, who had been listening on the phone extension.

"Well," I said, "I guess there's nothing for me to do but go out and look for the well and the pump and maybe it's just a fuse blown out or something."

I went outside and began to explore the property. Not far from the back door I came upon a circular cement cap set in the ground with an old-fashioned rusted hand pump protruding from it. I brightened considerably and set about wrestling the 200 pound cement cap off what was obviously a hole in the ground. I abrased my hands in the process and pulled innumerable small muscles in my back, but eventually I got the cap off. I looked down into the hole and my heart sank. The hole was lined with beautifully smooth obviously hand-carved stones and it was about sixteen feet deep. It no doubt was the original well put in by the original Wilkes some 250 years ago and a perfect example of the ingenuity and workmanship of the Connecticut pioneers. But there was no water in it.

I wrestled the cap back into place and resumed my search. I looked everywhere, but there was no well to be found. In my depressed mood, however, I saw many other foreboding things which had escaped my attention in the glow in which we had bought the house. The drainpipe around the edge of the roof was sagging and obviously in disrepair; the paint was peeling badly on the south side of the house, which was away from the main entrance and which we had never closely examined; the forest had jumped the stone fence behind the house and was encroaching voraciously on our lawn; the timbers were rotting on the inside of a decorative old-oaken-bucket well house which perched uselessly in the middle of our parking area.

I swung my fist at the old oaken bucket in helpless

fury and badly bruised my knuckles. As I trudged wearily back to the house, I tripped over a row of crumbling cement blocks which lined the driveway and badly bruised my naked toes. I walked into the house and I didn't have to tell Muriel and Carol of the fruitlessness of my mission. We just walked into the living room and sat there on the suitcases staring off into space. "What have we gotten ourselves into?" I said.

"I don't know, Blandings," said Muriel, "but the immediate question is what are we going to do now. I have to go to the bathroom."

I said, "In a few minutes, after my toes and knuckles stop hurting, I'm going to call Jay Morrow. Maybe he can tell me what to do, and at least he can let you use his bathroom." We resumed our sorry contemplation of the shambles in which we had found ourselves.

Just then we heard a tap on the back door and a cheery voice rang through the entire house. "Hello, there!" the cheery voice said.

I dragged myself to the door and a man was standing on the stone step. He was tall and built like a pro football linebacker and he wore a red shirt, blue jeans and workman's shoes. He was about forty years old and his face was ruggedly handsome and weatherbeaten. He thrust out a huge paw and I shook it limply. Trying to sound like what I thought the natives sounded like, I said, "Howdy!"

The man looked at me curiously upon my attempt at the local vernacular and he said, "I'm your neighbor, Steave Bjelko. Can I come in?" The name rang a remote bell in my brain but I couldn't connect it with anything and I waved him wearily inside.

He walked into the living room and I introduced him to Muriel and Carol, who were still sitting dejectedly on the suitcases. I saw a startled look come over his face as his eyes ran from one to the other of us and noted the chic yellow spots we all were wearing. I was too tired to explain.

Our visitor glanced quickly and expertly around the house and then the cheery voice boomed out again: "Are you folks having any trouble?"

None of us could bring ourselves to answer him. Muriel, however, emitted a bitter little laugh which gradually accelerated into the roar of merriment which is her trademark when something amuses her. Then Carol began to laugh—hysterically at first and then full-heartedly as she caught the contagion from Muriel. Finally I began to laugh, too.

Bjelko stood there looking at us as if we were all crazy.

chapter iv

Suddenly I remembered why our neighbor's name had struck a responsive chord when he introduced himself. After we had bought the house, Jay Morrow, the real estate agent, had said, "There's a feller lives next door to you, down the road about a quarter of a mile. Nice feller. Can do almost anything. But he's funny. He'll come over and if he likes you he'll help you out with any kind of problems you might have with the house. If he doesn't like you, he'll walk away and you might never see him again. Name's Bjelko, Steave. Spells it S-t-e-a-v-e. If you ask me why, I can't tell you."

As all this came back to me, my own hysterical reaction vanished instantaneously and I said pointedly to Muriel, "Darling, you remember. This is the Mr. Bjelko Jay Morrow told us about." Understanding dawned on Muriel's face and recovering her composure as quickly as I did, she shut Carol up by kicking her in the shin behind one of the suitcases. Carol abruptly decided to become the epitome of seventeen-year-old female charm. Using a combination Bryn Mawr-Deborah Kerr accent she was affecting at that time, she advanced on the stony-faced but obviously bewildered Bjelko and said, "Oh, Mr. Bjelko, *do* forgive us but we're a family that likes to lahf a lot. We're really chahmed to meet you because we heard that you would help us if you liked us."

I could see the groan on Muriel's face followed by a quick recovery as she looked out the window and noticed a beautiful Dalmatian sitting in the cab of Steave's truck, which he had parked in the driveway. "Oh, look at Mr. Bjelko's beautiful Dalmatian out there," she said to Carol. "You know how you love Dalmatians and you haven't seen one in months. Maybe Mr. Bjelko will let you go out there with him and pet the dog."

"But I don't love Dalmatians. I love Great Danes," said Carol.

"Oh, no, darling, you're confused," said Muriel, administering a severe tweak to the flesh of Carol's arm from the rear. "Dalmatians are those darling white dogs with black spots and you know how you just *loved* them when we went to the dog show."

"Oh, yes," said Carol. "Could I please go out and meet your dog and pet him, Mr. Bjelko?"

"Sure," said Steave, and he and Carol disappeared through the back door.

The minute we heard the door close, I hissed to Muriel, "For God's sake, we've *got* to make him like us. But don't make the mistake of asking him directly for help. Jay told me that would be just the wrong approach. We've got to get him to a point where he volunteers to help us himself."

"Roger," said Muriel.

The back door opened again and in came Steave and Carol and the Dalmatian, whose name was Boots. The dog sped wildly over the uncarpeted floors. He leaped upon us, knocked over suitcases and we all petted him and said what a beautiful animal he was. While I got down on the floor and allowed Boots to walk back and forth on me, alternately licking my face and my bare feet, Muriel got Carol aside in the bathroom and briefed her. During their absence I tried to convince Steave what a dog lover I was. I told him about the Irish Setter named Patsy I had had as a boy, about the Old English Sheepdog named Digby with whom I used to wrestle when I was in college and who used to pin me two falls out of three, and I even made up a total lie about an Irish Wolfhound named Ian who swam out into the Irish Sea and rescued me from an attacking dolphin. "I don't favor any kind of dog but the Dalmatian," said Steave.

I was just about to make up a sensational story about a Dalmatian saving me in a burning warehouse, when Muriel and Carol returned. They had both removed the yellow paint from their faces—although their clothing still had the polka-dot effect—and they looked charming. Muriel offered Steave a cup of coffee but he shook his head and said, "No, thanks. I have to get back to my wife, Janie." A look of desperation flitted across Muriel's eyes and she said, "Oh, you and Janie live in that beautiful modern house down the road. She must be a wonderful housekeeper. It always looks so clean and fresh when we drive past it."

"Yes," said Steave, "it's a *new* house. Built most of it myself." He looked around deprecatingly. "Never could understand why folks should want to buy an old house when they can have a new house."

"You're right," said Muriel. "There are so many problems with these old houses and—" I broke in, laughing hollowly, "Don't *hint*, dear, or Mr. Bjelko will think . . ." I ended the sentence in an unintelligible mumble.

"Well," said Steave, getting to his feet from the suitcase on which he had been sitting, "I been holdin' you folks up. I better get goin'." He shook hands solemnly with each of us, rounded up Boots, who was sniffing the place where the field mice had eaten the jelly beans, and he left.

We sat there plunged in uncontrollable gloom. "Well, we really blew *that*," said Carol, forgetting, for the moment, her Bryn Mawr-Deborah Kerr accent. I nodded and got up to phone Jay Morrow to tell him he'd better put the house back on the market again. As I reached the phone, it began to ring. "Now who would call us here?" said Muriel. I picked up the phone and there was the cheery "Hello, there!" again. Steave said, "I was just talkin' to my wife, Janie, and she said for you folks to come over and have a cup of coffee with us and see what we did with our *new* house."

"Be right over," I said, trying to act as casual as possible.

Our gloom underwent an instant change to manic hilarity as we rushed to change our paint-spattered clothes. "Maybe he likes us after all," Muriel said. "I don't know," I said, "but at least we've got another chance with him. This time, for God's sake, remember what Jay Morrow said and don't hint that we're in trouble and need him."

We got in our car and drove the quarter of a mile down the road to the Bjelko house. It was a neat gray ranch-style set up on the side of the mountain from the road and there were flower beds all around, giving it pleasant touches of color. We went in and met Janie, a pretty little woman with red hair like Muriel's, which Muriel immediately noted and commented upon. Steave took us around and proudly showed us the large plate-glass picture window in the living room, the electric organ, which he played for us briefly, the sparkling new appliances in the sparkling new kitchen and sparkling new basement. "Why *didn't* we get a new house?" Muriel said to me reproachfully.

We had coffee with the Bjelkos and we learned that he was of Bohemian descent, that he had been born and raised on a farm down the road, that he was a steam fitter by trade, that he was a member of the Town Zoning Board and President of the King Street Volunteer Firehouse. We learned that Janie was of pure Yankee stock, that her ancestors had bought the town of Ridgefield from the Indians, that she worked as a volunteer in a New Haven veterans' hospital, and that she was President of the Ladies' Auxiliary of the King Street Volunteer Firehouse. When Steave asked me what *I* did for a living, I was hesitant about telling him I earned my bread by tapping out stories on the typewriter like a lady stenographer, so I said, "I'm sort of in the publishing game." "Oh," he said, "advertising and printing and like that." "Yes," I said and darted to another subject.

Suddenly Carol started crying. "Well," I thought to myself, "we've really blown it now." I slumped in my chair while Muriel and Janie rushed over to see what was the matter. "Here it comes," I said to myself. Janie had her arms around Carol in a tender, motherly gesture and was saying, "Now come on, dear, tell us what's the matter." Carol sobbed for a few minutes more and burst out, "I have to go to the bathroom."

Janie looked puzzled. "That's all right, dear," she said, "the bathroom's just down the hall."

Muriel glowered at me. By now *her* motherly instincts had superseded anything else, and I knew the battle was lost. She said to Janie, "Please forgive Carol, but we don't have any water in our house. The pump isn't working or something."

Steave leaped to his feet and I said to myself, "Here it comes."

Steave said, "You mean you folks are having *trouble* over there?" I nodded weakly. He said, "Then let's you and I go over and leave the ladies to talk."

I followed Steave numbly to his truck and down the road to our house. In a matter of minutes he had found the well and pump, which were under the floor of what

I thought was just a decorative old-oaken-bucket well house and which I had passed a hundred times in my search. Down in the well, he discovered that the pump was a decrepit relic on its last legs, but he patched it up to run temporarily and phoned a plumber to come out with a new pump. It didn't even bother me that the new pump would cost three hundred and fifty dollars.

Next, Steave went into the house and set out traps and pellets to rid us of the field mice. "Won't bother you tonight," he said matter-of-factly.

With the mice taken care of, I followed him admiringly into the bedroom with the ballooning wallpaper and the evil green eyes peering through the yellow paint. "I got some stickum tape in the truck," he said. While I wondered what he was going to do with stickum tape, he went out and fetched it and began to run it along the seams where the wallpaper had come apart. Soon the tattered-looking walls were in one piece again, although the tapes gave them a bizarre, prison-window look. "Now," said Steave, "we paint a second coat over the walls, tapes and all." We both seized brushes and rollers and in about an hour the room was bright yellow and intact.

As we washed out our brushes and rollers under the merrily running tap in the kitchen sink, Steave looked at me sternly.

"If you were having trouble," he asked, "why didn't you say so?"

chapter v

The Bjelkos became our guides in our strange new rural world. Soon we were speaking the patois of the neighborhood. We were saying "Ey-eh" for "Yes"; we were adding the expression "onto it and all" to sentences, as in "I like my Wheaties with sugar onto it and all," or in variations like "He was taken to the hospital and they operated onto him and all"; going into town was "going downstreet"; "the snow is settling" was "the snow is making," etc. We gorged ourselves on Janie's apple pies and New England boiled dinners, and a jug of Steave's hard cider always sat on our bar next to the Scotch and vodka. Even Naomi got into the swing of it and she kept phoning Janie about recipes for New England-style braised short ribs, and the like. Once Muriel heard our middle-aged Panamanian belle discussing a dish for which she was listing such ingredients as pimento, saffron, sliced olives and garlic sausage. "What kind of New England dish is *that?*" asked Muriel. Naomi, whose sense of history and geography is sometimes garbled, replied with indignation, "When the Spanish settle here in the early days, this is the way they make fish and I am teaching Miss Janie."

Naomi has a tendency to sing while she is at work. In the city apartment her favorite vocals are the Cuban-rumba version of "Siboney" and "Double Your Pleasure, Double Your Fun" from the jingle in the Doublemint gum TV commercial. In the country house, she sang such numbers as "The Battle Hymn of the Republic" and, for some reason known only to her, "Taps." She persisted in her ambition to tend a cow and chickens in the back forty and when she could get nowhere with me in this resolve, she cannily planted a corn patch "for to make tortillas." The corn thrived, but by the time the ears had matured, Naomi was so thoroughly New Englandized that she served them roasted in the husk as she had seen Janie do.

We had bought the house in June and Muriel and Carol spent most of the summer buying furniture and gimcracks for it. Since our treasury was somewhat depleted by now, Muriel found that she couldn't afford to furnish the entire house in genuine Colonial antiques as she had planned. Never daunted by such handicaps as lack of money, Muriel thereupon hit on what she thought was a brilliant scheme. She said, "I'm going to buy one expensive antique which will go in the most conspicuous spot in the living room where it will catch everyone's eye the minute they walk in. They will be so overwhelmed by this authentic antique that they'll think everything else is authentic, too. But everything else will be reproductions."

She then went out and bought a magnificent gold Midas mirror from a couple of mincing Clairol-blond young men who sold their wares in a barn nearby. She mounted the mirror on the mantel over the fireplace and then set about buying the rest of our furnishings from such purveyors of pseudo-Americana as Bloomingdale's. The house ended up looking like a transplanted dwelling from the Colonial Williamsburg Restoration in Virginia, but Muriel's plan met with only mixed success. She completely fooled our sophisticated New York friends when they came to visit. As she had predicted, they took one look at the Midas mirror and were immediately convinced that everything else was almost as old as the house itself.

With our new-found Yankee friends, however, it was a different matter.

Janie brought over some of the members of the Ladies' Auxiliary of the King Street Firehouse one afternoon to have tea with Muriel. They ooh-ed and ah-ed over the pseudo-Americana and they asked Muriel where she had found such marvelous reproductions. Muriel became more and more crestfallen as the tea-drinking went on. She tried all stratagems to call attention to the Midas mirror and finally one of the ladies got up to scrutinize it. "Did you buy that mirror from a couple of pretty boys in New Milford?" the lady asked.

"Why, yes," said Muriel.

"They sure do a beautiful job there," the lady said. "They bought the original of this mirror from my sister, who inherited it from her mother-in-law, and they make such good copies that they sell them to the New York trade as originals."

I could not control a snicker, which Muriel unfortunately saw, and when the ladies had gone she hit me.

My own problems, usually of a mechanical or manual nature, continued unabated. Steave came over one night, for example, and I suggested that we watch a New York Yankees baseball game on television. Steave went over to the television set to turn it on and I shouted, "Don't do that." Startled, he said, "Why not?"

"Because," I said, "I have to do a few things first."

Then, while he watched in total amazement, I disconnected the refrigerator, an electric clock, and two lamps "OK, you can put the TV set on now," I said.

"Why did you do all that?" he asked.

"Because," I said, "if we use more than one appliance at a time in this house, the fuses blow out." He nearly doubled up with laughter and I asked, "Aren't *all* old houses like that?"

"Only if you keep on using the wiring that was put in fifty years ago. I'll get you an electrician to rewire the house."

So two weeks and three hundred dollars later our house was electrified for the uses of the mid-twentieth century, which meant—as the evidence of my own eyes told me—that Carol was able to dry her hair, listen to her record player, turn on her electric blanket, refresh her gums with her electric toothbrush and have all the lights blazing in her room, all at the same time. Our electric bill immediately went up five dollars a month.

I was having troubles on the *outside* of the house, too. Throughout the summer, I had desultorily mowed the lawns immediately surrounding our abode, but I chose to ignore the jungle that was developing further up the mountain. One day Steave said to me sternly, "You better do something about that, kiddo, or the poison ivy will be climbing in your back porch." The next day I dutifully ascended what had been the back lawn and began hacking away at the junior-grade forest. I chopped down saplings until my back ached and then I hit on a bright idea. There were a lot of dead leaves from the preceding fall and I thought it would be much easier to burn the debris than haul it away. So I built a neat little pile and set it afire.

In a matter of seconds, as I watched in stunned fascination, a little circle of flames had shot out from my pile and I was surrounded by a six-inch-high wall of fire about ten feet in diameter. I beat at the flames on one side of the circle with my hoe and then I jumped on them with my booted feet. The fire went out easily enough and I then did the same thing on the other side of the circle. But when I turned around the circle had reestablished itself. Muriel looked out the kitchen window and shouted at me, "Is everything all right, dear?" "Sure," I said, and I went back to my beating and jumping.

Suddenly I realized everything *wasn't* all right. The

circle was growing and the flames by now were licking up the stone wall, on the other side of which was the *senior*-grade forest. I was jumping at the flames so frenziedly that I kept falling down on the steep hillside. After I had fallen for about the eighth time, I roared, "Mu-ri-el!" My wife's face popped into the kitchen window again and she shouted, "I can't see you, dear. Are you in trouble?" "Yes," I roared. "Get Steave."

In about two minutes Steave and Janie came running over the rim of the hillside. Each was armed professionally with a shovel. They attacked the circle of flames with shovels of dirt and then Steave hopped the wall into the forest to take care of the leaves burning there. Just as he reappeared over the wall, Muriel arrived with her little watering can filled with water asking if there was anything she could contribute. Steave ignored her and turned to me. "What are you trying to do, burn down the mountain?" he said. After that he got his nephew Aaron to take care of the grounds for us. He didn't even ask me if I wanted Aaron. "I'm *giving* him to you," he muttered, "in self-defense."

But the worst of our problems were those that developed when we didn't have Steave and Janie around to help us solve them. Usually these originated in New York, where, because of our work, we spent about two days a week in our apartment. One day I came home to the apartment and Muriel met me, weeping, at the door. "Don't go in there," she moaned. "Why can't I go in there?" I said. "I live there."

"You won't want to when you see what I've done," she sobbed.

I walked down the short hall to the living room, turned the corner, and an astounding sight met my eyes. There, in the midst of our utilitarian, modern city furniture stood five enormous paper-wrapped bundles that looked like eight-foot-high syringes standing on their rubber bulbs. "My God," I said, "what are they?"

"They're trees," Muriel said.

"I know it's a silly question," I said, "but what are trees doing on our nice white carpet in our nice white living room?"

"Because I ordered them, that's why," she said.

"You ordered *trees* for the *living room*?" I said.

"No," she wept, "I ordered them for the country. For the driveway. They're Lombardy poplars. I saw them in a tree-nursery catalogue and it said they could only be delivered express collect and we're not in the country all the time and there's always a doorman here to accept them so I had them sent here. But how did I know they were so *big*?" She broke down again into enormous sobs.

An hour later, after I had stopped yelling, we sat down to figure out how we were going to get five eight-foot-tall Lombardy poplars out of our living room and up to the country where they belonged.

Finally I hit upon a plan. I went downstairs and consulted with Frank, the doorman, who lives in the country in New Jersey and knows about trees and stuff like that. When Frank went off duty early in the evening, he came up to our apartment and helped me tie the five poplars together into one bundle. Now they looked like an even bigger syringe. Frank and I then wrestled the enormous package to the freight elevator, first removing a plate in its roof so the tops of the poplars could protrude through (as the expressmen had done earlier) and somehow we got the bundle of trees to my car in the garage.

In those days of our ignorance (we later bought a station wagon) our car was a very sporty convertible. Frank said, "It's raining out. Do you want to ride wet or dry?"

"Dry," I said.

"Too bad," said Frank. "It would be easier with the top down."

We unzipped the rear window of the car and worked the root clumps of the trees through it so that they rested on the back seat. The trunks then shot up out of the rear window like a flagpole at a forty-five degree angle. "You can't ride like that," said Frank. "You'll get caught on bridges and things." He thought for a minute. "What kind of trees did you say they were?" he asked.

"Populars," I said (that's what the natives seem to call them in both Connecticut and New Jersey).

"Populars bend a lot in the wind, don't they?" asked Frank. I nodded. "Then it won't hurt if *we* bend them a little, eh?" Before I could answer, he had seized the lashed-together trunks, forced them down into a sweeping arc from where they were anchored by their root clumps on the back seat inside the rear window, and he tied the tips of the trunks with rope to the rear bumper of the car. "OK?" he said. "Fine," I said glumly, and I gave him the five-dollar bill I had nervously been twisting around my finger. "I'll send Mrs. Davidson down," he said. And he disappeared into the building.

Muriel came down and made the sort of disparaging remarks I was prepared for, like "Dig the bull whip," and "If that catapult breaks loose, our bumper will hit Montreal."

"Do you have any other ideas about how to do it?" I asked.

"No," she said.

"OK, then," I said. "Let's go."

We got in the car and I drove furtively up the East River Drive. The rain was pelting down and most of the drivers who passed us were too occupied trying to see out of their windshields to notice the strange protuberance at the back of our car. The rain, in the meantime, was blowing in the open rear window of our car and sprinkling the back of our necks.

I got out of the city on the Major Deegan Expressway and the New York Thruway, and in Westchester County I turned off onto the Saw Mill River Parkway. The rain had let up by now and there were few drivers; also, the Parkway was totally dark except for the occasional headlights, for which I was grateful. Just south of the Hawthorne Circle, I noticed the headlights of a car trailing us at about two hundred feet. As I looked in my rear-view mirror, I suddenly saw a flashing red light on the car's roof and we heard the unmistakable sound of a siren. The car pulled up alongside and in it was the unmistakable outline of a cop. He waved to me to stop at the side of the road, which I did. He pulled up in front of us with his car at an angle to block any attempt at escape. He got out of his car and advanced toward us with his hand on the holster of his revolver.

The policeman peered in my window and then slowly circled our car. He stopped after one full revolution and beckoned to me to get out. Still watching me warily with his hand on his holster, he walked with me to the rear of the car and asked, "What the *hell* is that?"

"That's trees," I said.

"You're putting me on," said the cop.

"No," I said. "It's really trees. Poplars."

"Poplars?" he asked.

"Populars," I said.

"Oh," he said. "Populars, a kind of a tree."

"That's what I told you," I said.

"Don't get cute, Mac," he said, and he walked over to the lashed-down poplar trunks and felt them. He took out a pocket knife and cut the paper in which the tree trunks were wrapped. Then he walked over to the side window of the car and flashed his light on the back seat and on Muriel, who for one of the few times in her life remained mute.

He came back to me and I started to explain about Muriel and the tree-nursery catalogue, and how we had to get the populars out of our living room and up to the country, but I stopped in the middle of my recitation, realizing I was not getting through to him. "Just stand where you are, Mac," the cop said, and he walked over to his own car. I could overhear him talking on the radio: "This joker says it's a bundle of trees but it looks like one of them high-powered portable radio transmitters to me. The goddam antenna is ten feet long and as thick as your leg. Wouldn't be surprised if they could reach Cuba with it. Maybe something for the FBI. . . . OK, I'll bring 'em in."

Without getting out of his car, the cop yelled at me, "OK, Mac, get in your car and drive to Westchester Parkway Police Headquarters, about a mile up the road on the left. I'll be right behind you, so don't try anything funny."

We drove to the police station and three other cops were waiting for us outside. While we sat in the car, they walked around and poked at the trees and conferred. Then a man in overalls came out and sliced the paper off the tip of the bundle. He made Muriel and me get out of the car and he slit the paper off the root clumps on the back seat. "It's trees," he announced to the others, and he went back into the building.

The cop who had arrested us talked to the other policemen for a moment and then he came over and asked for my driver's license and car registration. He began to write a summons. "What's *that* for?" I asked. "You violated a state law," he said. "You're not supposed to drive on a parkway with anything protruding more than a foot from the back of the car and them goddam trees are sticking out fourteen inches." I began to remonstrate with him, but Muriel poked me in the ribs and I shut up. The cop finished writing and said, "Since you come from out of town, you can mail the fine in.

(49)

It'll be ten dollars." He started to walk away but turned back. "And another thing," he added. "Get that load off the parkways and stay off."

The rest of the trip was even more of a nightmare. We had to drive through all the little towns between Hawthorne, New York, and Danbury, Connecticut, and we lost our way a half dozen times. The trip, which should have taken an hour and a half, stretched out to nearly four hours. At each of the dozens of traffic lights at which we had to stop, someone would yell in the window, "Hey, what's that sticking out of the back of your car?" At first I said trees, but this only led to incredulity and more questions, so about the twentieth time I coolly said, "It's one of them high-powered portable radio transmitters, Mac." I found that this worked. The questioner invariably nodded knowingly at my answer and lapsed into respectful silence.

We finally got home at about 1 A.M. We were both exhausted. We left the car and started to go into the house, but Muriel said, "Those poor trees with their little heads bent over all this time. Why don't you cut them loose from the bumper so at least they can straighten up by morning?"

"Good thinking," I said. I took out my Boy Scout knife and slashed cavalierly at the rope which bound the tops of the trees to the bumper. There was a sound like a hundred bows twanging loose their arrows, and I watched in horror as the bundle of tree trunks shot upright, slammed against the top of the open rear window of the car and then continued onward, ripping its way through about ten inches of the cloth roof of the convertible.

"How much is a new convertible roof, dear?" Muriel said.

Benumbed, I answered matter-of-factly, "Only about a hundred dollars, dear."

We left the trees sticking up through the roof of the car like a mast on a sailing vessel and tottered in to bed.

The next morning Steave came over to help me plant the trees. I was ashamed to let him see the torn roof, so by the time he got there, I had wrestled the trees out of the car myself and had hidden the car in the garage. Steave unwrapped the bundle of trees and examined them professionally. "Dead," he observed dryly. "Probably dead on arrival. That happens in shipping."

"Oh, *no*," we said.

"Can't understand why you had them shipped all the way from Michigan," he said. "You can buy populars like this just down the road for a dollar apiece."

chapter vi

One day, a little later in the summer, I was at work at my typewriter in one of the upstairs rooms when I happened to look out the window and I saw Steave in our driveway, practicing what seemed to be golf swings. "That's strange," I thought to myself, knowing that the only sport Steave participated in was bowling, every Tuesday and Friday night. Besides, he was swinging with a rake, not a golf club.

Since any excuse to avoid work was always welcome, I rushed downstairs and caught up with Steave as he walked across the road, the rake held out in front of him. "What's up, old buddy?" I asked. "This," he said laconically, and he gestured with his free hand toward the end of the rake. A two-foot dead snake was dangling limply from the implement. "Where did *that* come from?" I asked.

"Where did it *come* from?" said Steave with the mixture of amusement and disgust with which he often treated my stupid questions. "You're in Connecticut, kiddo," he said, "and in Connecticut there are millions of stone fences and in the millions of stone fences live lots and lots of these fellers. In a way, I guess you could say it's *their* country. They were here before folks was."

"What is it?" I asked eagerly. "Copperhead? Rattlesnake?"

"Nah," he muttered, "just a little ole garter snake. That's all we got around here, except maybe down in the swamps near the reservoir." He then proceeded to tell me a horrendous tale, probably untrue, about whole families getting wiped out by the copperheads years ago while picnicking on the banks of the reservoir.

As he recounted the hair-raising story, he disposed of the carcass of the snake in the woods across the road and we headed back to the house. Fascinated, I asked, "Where did that particular snake live?"

"Hard to tell," said Steave. "They come and go, lookin' for food, but this feller probably belongs to that nest of 'em that hangs out in that stone wall just behind your back porch." At that, the hackles rose on my neck, not because I have anything against harmless little garter snakes, but because I suddenly remembered that Muriel has a mortal fear of serpents of any kind or description, no matter how sedate they might be (she had once fled screaming from the home of a friend of ours in Massachusetts when an oversize earthworm

(53)

popped unexpectedly out of the lawn after a heavy rain).

"Steave," I said, "you've got to promise me something."

He looked at me suspiciously. "What?" he asked.

"You've got to promise me," I continued, "that you'll never tell Muriel about the snakes in the fence behind the porch, otherwise she'll leave here and never come back and she'll make me sell the house."

Steave looked puzzled, but he said, "OK."

"Not only that," I said, "but you've got to help me get rid of the snakes."

"How are you going to do *that?*" he said. "The snakes *live* here. Might just as well try to get rid of the bumblebees."

"Sh!" I said. "She's afraid of *them,* too. Did you ever try to get rid of garter snakes before?"

"Why *should* I?" he said. "I just kill one every once in a while because I don't like them, but they're good to have around. They eat the mice and things like that. Better than keeping a cat."

I thought for a moment. "Well," I said, ignoring the basic common sense of Steave's biological reasoning, "I'm sure science has found *some* way of getting rid of snakes. I'll check and let you know."

He shrugged and hoisted the rake onto his shoulder. "My lands, I better go now," he said. "Janie must just about have my supper ready." This was his usual method of dismissing me when he felt I had taken leave of my senses.

The next morning I phoned a friend of mine, a veterinarian at the Bronx Zoo, and told him my problem. I detected weariness in his voice as he informed me he had been up all night with a sick baby hippopotamus. "I'll call you back," he said. "But you don't even know where I am," I said. "That's all right," he said. And he hung up.

That approach having obviously failed, I went to see my friend Earl Taylor, who owns a hardware-and-garden store in the village of New Fairfield. Earl, a former cop in the town of Bethel, had previously been an unfailing source of information for me, on subjects ranging from local gossip to how to preserve begonia bulbs over the winter. I told him about the snakes. "What do you want to get rid of the snakes for?" he said. "They eat mice. Better than having a cat around." I explained about Muriel's reptile phobia.

"Well," said Earl, "I read in *National Geographic* about a bird in Egypt called the ibis that eats snakes. Maybe you could get one of those."

I said, "Isn't there a spray or something?"

"Dunno," said Earl, "but I'll find out."

He picked up the phone and called the County Agricultural Agent. He detailed my plight to the government man. I heard Earl say, "Yeah, I told him they were better than having a cat around." He spoke a few minutes longer and after he had hung up he said, "Twenty-five percent DDT."

"DDT?" I said. "I thought that's for ants and bugs. How can it kill snakes?"

"At twenty-five percent," Earl said, "it can kill *you*."

"Hmm," I said. I left Earl's with a jar of the potent DDT solution.

The next day, Steave and I went to work. We sprayed every nook and cranny of the hundred-foot stone wall with a foul-smelling liquid. Dead wasps, hornets, spiders, grasshoppers and other unidentifiable creatures by the hundreds came tumbling out of the gaps between the loosely piled-up rocks. But no snakes. "Maybe they thrive on this stuff," said Steave.

For the next month, we regularly sprayed the wall every few days with absolutely no visible effect. A couple of times, Muriel peered out of the back porch and asked what we were doing. "Oh, just waterproofing the wall, darling," I'd say. "But why?" she'd ask. "Can water go through rocks?" "No," I'd say, "but when the fall rains come, the water can go *between* the rocks and maybe flood our basement." That explanation, thought up in advance by Steave, seemed to pacify Muriel and she always went back unconcernedly to what she was doing.

When we continued to see no snake cadavers I said hopefully to Steave, "Maybe they go away to die, like elephants."

He said, "Nope. They're still in the wall."

I said, "How do you know?"

He said, "Because I killed three of 'em yesterday. By the old-fashioned method. The rake."

That evening I found out he was right. At the end of the wall there was a built-in stone barbecue which I no longer used because of the danger of the DDT residue. I had set up a portable grill next to it, however. I went out to broil some steaks on the portable grill and as I worked I had a feeling someone was watching me. I looked up and there was a snake, basking in the heat from the portable grill and lying on the ancient well stone which made up the top of the built-in barbecue. The snake was staring at me with his beady little eyes, and when I turned around he disappeared nonchalantly into the DDT-drenched wall.

After that, we had a series of Keystone Kop situations in our attempts to keep Muriel from learning our secret. One afternoon, while she was taking the sun on the back lawn, Steave came over with his dog, who, in prancing about, stepped on a snake and disabled it. I place-kicked the snake into the woods an instant before Muriel looked up from her book to see what I was doing. Another time, Naomi came upon one of the snake brethren while she was out in back hanging up the wash. Since such confrontations were commonplace to her in her native country, she calmly killed the reptile and was bringing it, dangling, to show me, just as Muriel started out the back door of the house. I practically tackled Naomi, thrusting her behind the garage in the nick of time. I smoothed Naomi's ruffled dignity, explained the situation to her, and swore her to silence about her kill. The next morning, I heard a scream from Carol out on the back lawn. Turning on all my speed, I got to her a few seconds before Muriel did. Carol said to me, "I saw a—" I didn't let her finish the sentence.

Rolling my eyes and shaking my head, I said, "You saw *anything* but a snake, dear." Muriel arrived. Carol said, "I saw a—a porcupine." Muriel said, "Is *that* all, dear?" And she went calmly back into the house.

By now, everyone knew the secret of the snakes but Muriel. The rest of us developed a clandestine speech technique in talking to each other about them. Steave would say, "I saw another one of your friends today." I referred to them as "the little rascals." Naomi called them *"los diablitos"* (the little devils). Carol mischievously thought up all sorts of euphemisms, such as "I ran into Uncle Wiggly out for his morning slither."

Finally Steave and I decided that we were losing the war of attrition against the reptiles and that we had to plan a grand final offensive. "There's only one thing to do," said Steave.

"What's that, try to find another Saint Patrick?" I said.

Steave ignored this riposte. "We've got to cement up the wall behind the house," he said.

"The *whole* wall?" I said. "My God, it's a hundred feet long."

"I know," said Steave, "but you and Aaron and I can do it on a Saturday."

The following Saturday we went to work at the backbreaking task of resetting the stones and smearing cement into the thousands of gaps between them. It took us all day—principally because my sacroiliac gave out—and part of Sunday. When she saw us working on the wall, Muriel said, "What are you doing, dear?" I laughed gaily and said, "The waterproofing, darling. Remember?" "Oh, yes," she said and ignored us thenceforth.

After the wall was cemented up, the snakes indeed disappeared. The following Sunday Steave and I were complimenting ourselves on our triumph when I looked up and saw Muriel hurrying toward us in a panic from one of her flower beds, a couple of hundred feet away. "Oh, oh," I said.

"Do you know what I saw near the flower bed?" she said.

She was white-faced but not hysterical. This encouraged me and I asked, "What did you see near the flower bed, dear?"

"A snake skin"—she shuddered—"and where there are snake skins there are snakes."

I figured the jig was up and she wasn't carrying on the way I had expected her to, so I decided to tell her the whole story, ending with the glorious victory we had scored by cementing the wall. Her eyes grew stony and she looked at me through ominous little slits.

She said, "Do you mean to tell me you used gallons of DDT on that wall right near the house?"

"Yes," I said, "and it didn't work."

"You idiot," she said.

"Idiot . . . idiot?" I asked.

"Yes," she said. "Didn't you read *Silent Spring?* Didn't you see all that Rachel Carson testimony to Congress about poisoning our water and our food? And how about destroying the balance of nature?"

I could not answer.

Neither could Steave.

He said, "My lands, I better go now. Janie must just about have my supper ready."

chapter vii

Integrating ourselves into the life of the community was easier, in a way, than segregating ourselves from the lives of our resident reptiles. Muriel, being gregarious and a big mouth by nature (especially in stores and markets), soon got to know many of our neighbors for miles around. She also quickly became a member of the Ladies' Auxiliary of the King Street Volunteer Firehouse, under Janie's auspices. As my wife whipped off to the Ladies' Auxiliary meetings dressed in cotton skirt and blouse, I thought of the chic career girl Muriel Davidson of New York and Hollywood, and I wondered what the maître d's at her favorite big-city restaurants would say if they could see her now.

Once, I stopped by at the firehouse to pick her up after one of the meetings. The session was still on and as I poked my head into the back room, I observed all the ladies staring at her with rapt attention, chin in hand, elbows on table, as she told them about the peccadilloes of the movie stars which she had observed at first hand when she was a publicity woman at Columbia Pictures. I had to wait for her closing story about how she helped put a stop to the romance between Kim Novak and Rafael Trujillo, Jr., the son of the Dominican Republic dictator. When she finally finished and we left the neat brick building, I said, "What the hell kind of firehouse business is *that?*" "Beats me," she said, "but that's what the ladies want to hear about."

Muriel had a ball at the firehouse. The fund-raising cake sales and barbecues came and went, and despite the demands made on the other ladies, Muriel was never asked to contribute a homemade pie or potato salad. Once I asked Janie why and she looked around furtively and said, "I always make *two* and put one in Muriel's name." One night at about 4 A.M., however, Janie phoned and said to Muriel, "You better hurry, dear. The men are all out fighting a big brush fire over near the New York State line. We need you to make sandwiches and coffee for them." Muriel, drugged with sleep, just stared at the phone and said something that sounded like, "Wah-wah-wah." I seized the phone and told Janie I'd give Muriel the message when she got up. Janie repeated the request, and then said, "Never mind. Just tell her I'll call her in the morning." In the morning Janie said to Muriel, "I guess we'll just have to consider you a prestige member."

Not long after we had bought the house, Muriel was padding around "downstreet" in Danbury in battered blue jeans, when she passed a book store called Bell, Book and Candle. Whenever a book of mine is published, Muriel puts into effect an economic theory peculiar only to her whereby she walks into every book store she encounters and purchases a copy of my book, the principle being that she only has to spend $3.95, say, to earn me sixty cents in royalties. In Bell, Book and Candle, she airily asked the clerk for *The Real and the Unreal*. The man brightened and said, "Oh, yes. Fine book." He lowered his voice confidentially. "The author," he said, "just moved into the neighborhood. Isn't that exciting? I saw his wife on TV the other day talking about the book. Beautiful woman. Beautifully dressed." Not at all fazed, Muriel bubbled happily, "That author is my husband and that wife is me!" She and the clerk then chatted merrily for about a half hour.

Perhaps it was coincidental, but after that conversation the phone began to ring at our house and total strangers requested our presence at various functions throughout the state. I, for example, was asked to address a group of Connecticut librarians at a luncheon in a YWCA in Bridgeport, which I did, telling the ladies lurid tales about my own Hollywood experiences—most of which I stole from Muriel's firehouse repertoire. Muriel was visibly annoyed at my plagiarisms but on such occasions she never counterattacks directly and usually takes out her aggressions with some diversionary thrust. This time she snarled, "How could you keep hitching up your pants in front of such prim ladies—and in a YWCA, too?" This was all I had to hear, being nervous about my presence in a YWCA to begin with.

At about the same time, Muriel was asked to deliver a speech to the state convention of the Insurance Women of Greater Connecticut in the town of Norwalk. The lady who phoned her said, "Faith Baldwin did it for us last year and all she asked for was a contribution to her favorite charity. This year we wanted Candy Jones, but she was too expensive." In a vast wave of magnanimity, Muriel, who always referred to the organization as "the Greater Ladies," said, "I will speak to you Greater Ladies for *nothing*." The Greater Lady on the phone was so stunned at this offer that she terminated the conversation abruptly so as not to give Muriel a chance to change her mind. "What did you do *that* for," I asked my mate. "Oh," she said airily, "a good neighbor always does things like that for nothing."

The nothing cost me plenty. There was a new dress that had to be bought, new shoes, hat, gloves, a hairdo and a pedicure (even though, as I insisted, her feet wouldn't show), and I had to pay for a new portrait for the newspapers (Muriel's last photos had been taken six months before and she said she didn't look like that any more). Muriel delivered a very creditable lecture on women and careers, and in appreciation the Greater Ladies gave her a bouquet of yellow roses. "You're the yellow-rose type, my dear," said one of the Greater

Ladies to my spouse. I beamed because I considered this to be pleasant lady-type conversation, the nuances of which I never seem to be able to grasp. I was wrong again. I saw Muriel's Celtic temper on the rise, the eyes narrowed and she said witheringly, "No, honey, I'm really the Venus's-flytrap type." She stormed out, with me behind her, and I said, "What was *that* all about?" She flicked a drop of rain off the sleeve of the new dress she had bought for the speech. "Men," she said, "are idiots."

Not long after that, Muriel got a telephone call from Dave Jowdy, a nice man we knew who owned the diner in New Fairfield where we frequently took lunch. Dave said, "Muriel, could you help us out? We need you and Bill to judge a beauty contest."

Muriel said, "A beauty contest? In the diner?"

"No," said Dave, "in the basement of the A & P. They got a hall there called the Fountain Room. You see, I'm an officer of the organization of Arabic-speaking peoples in Danbury and every year we have this three-day festival called the Mahrajan, and on the first night we have a beauty contest to pick the Queen of the Mahrajan."

"Arabs in Danbury?" asked Muriel.

"Yes," said Dave, "there are four thousand of us, maybe the biggest concentration in America. We got four churches—three Catholic and one Orthodox."

"How did the Arabs get here?" asked Muriel, fascinated.

"They came over in the old days to work in the Danbury hat factories," said Dave. "A lot of people in

Syria and Lebanon know how to process fur for felt. I think they wore felt underwear in the winter in the mountains in the old country."

Muriel giggled. She said, "Do you promise you won't put me in a harem or ship Bill to Cairo in a trunk?"

Dave, a cheery cosmopolitan man, giggled back. He said, "We Christian Arabs always told the Moslem Arabs they shouldn't do things like that."

"OK," said Muriel. "Bill and I will judge the beauty contest."

The next day we were visited by Mr. and Mrs. George Reimers, who were co-chairmen of the Mahrajan Ball. They told us we would be two of three judges (the third was Reimers' boss, a supermarket executive named O'Rourke) and that we had to pick the Queen not only for her beauty but also for her poise and for how well she represented the Arabic community. Mrs. Reimers was a handsome, motherly, dark-eyed woman, who if she had been wearing flowing robes instead of a neat suit-dress, could have stepped right out of *Scheherazade*. On the other hand, she might just as well have been the president of the local chapter of Hadassah. Talking with the Reimerses, it was forcibly brought back to me how closely related the embattled Jews and Arabs are. Mrs. Reimers looked so much like my Aunt Becky that she could have been her sister. She even spoke and thought like my Aunt Becky. Looking speculatively at Carol, she said, "Why don't you bring your daughter to the Mahrajan. Maybe she can meet a nice Lebanese boy there."

The Mahrajan Ball was on the Friday night of the

Labor Day weekend. While Muriel and I drove to the Fountain Room, a couple of miles away, I was overwhelmed by the spirit of the brotherhood of man as I realized that an Irishman, a Welshwoman and a Jew were about to select the local flower of Arabic young womanhood. Just in case there was an outburst of anti-Zionist sentiment, however, I carried my Boy Scout knife in my pocket.

It turned out, however, that it was not necessary for me thus to cover my bets. The Arabs were all warm and friendly and I recognized many of my friends and neighbors. Several of the people had Arabic names like Hajj and Buzaid, but many more had Americanized their names, which is why I had never suspected their Near Eastern origin. They were well dressed, and they danced the twist, and except for an occasional interlude of Arabic music played by four young men on ancient instruments like the lute, it might just as well have been an affair of the local Elks Club.

We boozed it up and ate Arabic delicacies and generally had a wonderful time. Then came the main event of the evening, the beauty contest. Muriel and O'Rourke and I went backstage with Abe Najamy, a local newscaster who was serving as master of ceremonies. Abe introduced us to the six contestants. As we looked at them, Muriel and I and O'Rourke stared at each other in consternation. Five of the girls were lithe, brunette, typically Eastern Mediterranean damsels; the sixth was a magnificent six-foot typically Nordic beauty. "What's *she* doing here?" Muriel asked Najamy.

"I was afraid you were going to ask me that," said Najamy. "Her mother is Lebanese. Her father is German. She looks like her father, but she was brought up as a Lebanese Catholic. She belongs to my church."

Muriel, who had had previous experience with such matters as beauty contests and whom O'Rourke and I acknowledged as our leader, called us into a hasty conference. She said, "If we were judging on looks alone, that big blond girl wins hands down and the ball game's over already. But remember, we've got an out. The girls have to answer questions about the careers they've chosen and about life and stuff like that. The blonde can't be that pretty and be smart, too, so I think we'll still have a chance to pick someone who looks more Arabic."

"OK," O'Rourke said, "we'll think Arabic."

We judges went back to the ballroom and sat at a table that had been set up in the middle of the dance floor. The orchestra played a fanfare on the lutes and Abe came out and introduced the girls one at a time. They then paraded around the dance floor in their pretty short-length evening dresses. Then, each girl in turn was brought up to the microphone and Abe asked her to pick three slips of paper out of a basket. On each slip of paper was written a question, prepared by Muriel, on such profound subjects as, "Do you think a woman can have a career and be a good wife and mother at the same time?" We were to judge the girls' poise by the way they answered the questions.

The five Arabic beauties came and went and a couple

of them answered their questions quite creditably. "Thank God," Muriel whispered to me. Then the blonde stepped to the microphone. She seized it with complete self-assurance and answered the questions in unfaltering, well-modulated tones, and with extraordinary intelligence. She explained that she was going to study to be a nurse because of her deep interest in science and medicine and because this was the only way open to her to serve suffering mankind. "Oh, brother," I said to Muriel. O'Rourke was perspiring. He said, "I'm trying to think Arabic, but that blonde's a mile ahead of the other girls. What are we going to do?"

I said, "There are two courses open to us. Either we play it square like umpires in a ball game and give it to the blonde, or we play it safe and be dirty rat finks." We sat there staring at each other miserably for a few minutes. Then we all voted for the blonde.

The blonde wept in traditional fashion and her mother came up and embraced her and she wept, too. Under cover of all the weeping, Muriel, O'Rourke and I slunk back into the crowd. Several people glowered at us, saying, "What kind of Lebanese is *that?*" or "What kind of Syrian is *that?*"

Muriel and I were afraid to face George Reimers and we were moving toward the door for an early exit. Suddenly, however, a tall, handsome Lebanese priest named Father Faris saved the day by walking up to Carol and asking her to join him in an Arabic folk dance in the middle of the floor. The muttering stopped and all the Arabs clustered around and said, "Ah, isn't that darling?" and things like that.

I hissed to Muriel "*You* get out there and dance too." I pushed her onto the floor and the next thing I knew she was doing a belly dance (a technique she learned once while posing as a showgirl in order to write an inside story for the *Saturday Evening Post* on the sad life of the vanishing chorine).

Everybody applauded and said how wonderful it was that a famous woman like Muriel should take the time to learn Arabic dances. Our perfidy in the beauty contest was forgotten and good fellowship reigned once again.

chapter viii

After the Mahrajan, the summer departed quickly up on our mountain. Soon we were enjoying the breathtaking autumn foliage, which in previous years we had only been able to admire from afar while driving as transients through the New England countryside. Carol—who had gone off to college and now was only an occasional weekend visitor—was unimpressed, but Muriel rushed around in our woods exulting, "It's mine, all mine." She came into the house with armfuls of red, yellow and orange leaves and marveled at the fact that in New York she would have had to pay a dollar to a florist for each branch. She went downstreet to Bell, Book and Candle and had her friend, the clerk, order her several books on how to preserve autumn foliage as permanent decorations for the house. Then she went to our pharmacist friend, Brian Burnell, and bought medical-grade glycerin and other concoctions in which to treat the foliage. With the books and the chemicals, I figured out that it was costing me about a dollar and a quarter a branch.

It wasn't until about the first of November that Muriel got tired of fooling around with the foliage and I sat back waiting to see what her next project would be. I guessed that it would be a toboggan slide or a bobsled run down the mountain through our woods, and with the days getting chillier, I mentally prepared myself for such a proposal. One Sunday afternoon, I knew it was coming. Muriel sat quietly on the couch, obviously deep in thought. Then she said, "Darling?" I said, smugly, "Yes, dear?" Muriel said, "Let's put in a swimming pool."

After about two minutes of stunned silence, I said, "Whom the gods would destroy, they first make mad."

"No," she said, "I've been reading a book, and it says this is the best time of the year to build a pool. It's cheaper because the pool builders aren't busy now."

I looked out the window at the north wind churning down the mountain. "I'll bet they aren't," I muttered. "What else does that book say?"

Muriel replied, "It says that you must be very careful about picking your pool builder because a lot of them go bankrupt and then you are stuck with no guarantee on your pool in case anything goes wrong."

"That clinches it," I said with finality. "No pool."

The next morning I was calling anyone I could think of who could possibly know anything about pools. I had succumbed, during the night, to various arguments, chief among them: (1) that I was getting too fat and exercising in a pool every day during the summer might save me from a coronary attack or worse; (2) our cash position had once again improved and what better way to spend the excess money; and (3) think of all the editors I could entertain at the pool and thus get myself many more magazine and book assignments.

After a lot of phone calls I finally got to a man named Marty who was a partner in a public relations firm that had a pool company as one of its clients. I had known Marty when I was a sports writer and he was a press agent for what later turned out to be crooked boxing bouts. "Sure I can get you a pool," said Marty. "Wholesale." He quoted a figure that was a thousand dollars lower than any other estimate I had received. I was ecstatic at this and said, "We've got a deal." I remembered the one question, however, that Muriel had insisted I ask: "Are you sure your pool company is stable and won't go bankrupt, leaving me with no guarantee on the pool in case anything goes wrong?"

"This firm," said Jerry, "is as solid as A.T.&T. They also build air-raid shelters for the government. I'll have our Connecticut franchise-holder come over to see you tomorrow."

The next day we were visited by a personable and handsome young man named Vito. The sign on his truck indicated that he was an installer and servicer of septic sewage tanks. "There must be some mistake," I said. "We want a swimming pool, not a septic tank." "I know," he said. "We also build swimming pools. That's another division of my company." "Oh," I said.

"Where do you want this pool?" said Vito.

"We thought it would be nice over there on the side lawn," said Muriel.

"Can't," said Vito. "The septic tank's under that lawn."

"How about the other side lawn?" I asked.

"No good," said Vito. "Too near the trees. Too much shade. Doesn't make sense to have a swimming pool in the shade."

"Where then?" I asked.

Vito walked about, scrutinizing the terrain professionally. "There's only one place," he said. "Right behind the house."

"But that's *mountain!*" Muriel exclaimed. "We don't want our pool on a slant."

"Don't worry," said Vito. "We take that part of the mountain away and level it off into a nice terrain. It won't cost you much extra. Just a couple of days' rental of my earth-moving equipment plus labor."

"What else is going to be extra?" I asked glumly.

"Well," said Vito, "are you going to go into your swimming pool directly from the ground with dirty feet?"

"I don't think so," I said.

"Then you'll need a patio all around the pool," he said. "That'll be extra."

He looked at a check list. "And how are you going to enter this pool?" he asked.

"By a diving board and a ladder, I guess," I said.

"Both extra," said Vito.

By the time we totaled up the extras, Muriel and I discovered that our wholesale pool was going to cost us about three hundred dollars less than the retail pools we had considered. "Oh, well," Muriel said, "it's *still* less, and Vito is such a nice young man. Why don't we sign the contract with him?"

So we signed the contract.

The next day Vito and his men began work. We soon learned that the five men with him all were his brothers. They started with their power shovel and the mountain commenced to disappear behind the house. A chill wind was whipping down the mountain and the men were bundled up in winter work clothes. Steave came by on his way home from his job, observed the activity for a minute and asked, "How's the skating rink coming along?"

After exchanging badinage with Vito and his men for a while, Steave came into the house with us. "What are you going to do about ledge?" he said.

"Ledge?" I asked. "I don't believe I know anyone named Ledge."

"No," said Steave. "Ledge *rock*. That's what this whole part of Connecticut is made of. It's the hard core of the earth. It sticks up everywhere. The old farmers chipped off chunks of it to make those stone fences. When you hit it, it might be miles deep. But that young feller doesn't seem to know that. I think he's used to working in that part of Connecticut where it's all sand, like where those rich folks live down in Westport."

I rushed out to see Vito. "What are you going to do about ledge?" I demanded.

"Nothing to worry about," said Vito cheerfully. "You see that stone fence behind the house that some damn fool cemented up? Well, it's all fill behind it." He showed me rusty horseshoes, dog bones, assorted barnyard debris, even a couple of old Indian arrowheads, that his power shovel was turning up in the soft earth behind the wall.

I went back into the house and reported this intelligence to Steave. "Hmm," he muttered. "Well, I better go home and get my supper now."

The days came and went and we had a wonderful time with Vito and his brothers. Muriel had hot coffee brewing for them throughout the day, and periodically they'd come into the kitchen to get out of the continuous chill wind. They brought huge sacks of doughnuts which they consumed with their coffee, and after the first day, they brought doughnuts for us, too. I discussed horticulture and politics with Vito, and he gave household hints to Muriel. He taught her, for example, never to scour an iron skillet. To me the excavating process was the most marvelous excuse I had ever had to keep from working. I was the only kid on my block who could be a sidewalk superintendent in my own back yard.

By the third day, however, I knew something was wrong. The power shovel was standing silent off to one side and deep in the excavation the men were pounding away with pickaxes and sledgehammers. "What's going on?" I shouted down to Vito. He looked up with a worried expression on his face. "Ledge," he said.

Remembering Steave's warning, I asked, "What are you going to do?"

"We'll do *something*," said Vito. "Maybe dynamite." I felt a twinge of apprehension but also a thrill of excitement at the expectation of real explosions just outside my window. My work was totally forgotten now as I watched the windows being taped up, the holes drilled in the hard ledge rock, the heavy mesh steel mats put in place over the explosive. Then came the blast. The house shook, four windows blew out—and only a few handfuls of loose rock fell away from the mass of ledge. "That's what I was afraid of," said Vito. "We're too close to the house to use big enough a blast. We'll have to go to jackhammers."

For five more days Muriel and I watched the men working with the power-driven jackhammers, and if anything, it was more fun than watching the explosion. They would find a seam in the rock and painstakingly work along it until the harder rock began to fall away. On the fifth day of the jackhammers, Vito said, "I hope you don't mind this."

Muriel bubbled, "Why should we *mind* it. It's fun."

Vito said, "I mean the extra expense onto it and all."

Instantaneously, it wasn't fun any more. I said, "You mean this is—er—extra?"

"Extra," said Vito. "It's in the contract. Clause about in case ledge is encountered."

"How *much* extra?" I asked.

"A hundred and fifty dollars a day," said Vito. I got the same sinking feeling I had once had in a dream in which I had been riding around the United States for a month in a chauffeur-driven Rolls-Royce and then the driver pulled back a panel in the dashboard and a taxi meter had been running all the time. "Call Steave," I said weakly to Muriel.

Steave came over and surveyed the situation. He crawled about in the excavation and then he said to Vito, "How much further you figurin' on cuttin' down into that ledge?"

"Oh, about another foot," said Vito.

"Well," said Steave, "how about raisin' the whole pool up another foot and don't cut any more. My lands, you're so far up the mountain already that another foot won't make any difference."

"Good idea," said Vito disconsolately.

After that, the pool was finished in record time. The walls went in, then the pump, the drains and the plumbing. On November eighteenth, Vito began filling the pool with water pumped by hose from both our new well and our old well simultaneously. He also brought huge tank trucks of water from Ball Pond, about a mile down the road. On November twentieth, the water was all in. Vito looked at his handiwork with satisfaction and said to us, "Well?"

"Well what?" said Muriel.

"It's the tradition," said Vito, "that when a pool is finished, the owners go into it—for the workmen. So they can see the ladies in bathing suits."

"Are you crazy?" I said. "It's November. The temperature can't be more than thirty-four degrees."

"If that's the tradition," said Muriel, "we're going in."

I was dragged off to our bedroom, where we both got into our bathing suits. Carol was home from college that weekend with a classmate named Nancy Matthews, and *they* got into their bathing suits, too. We then put on overcoats over our bathing suits and went out to the pool. While the workmen watched and applauded, Muriel, Carol and I dunked modestly up to our knees in the shallow end and then rushed benumbed into the house to recuperate. However, Nancy, a large, lusty, athletic country girl, made a totally unrestrained leap into the pool at about the four-foot level. She landed with one foot on the still soft bottom, leaving an ineradicable impression which to this day we still point out to sightseeing visitors as "Nancy Matthews' Footprint."

Later, while we were recovering our blood circulation before the fire, Vito came in and gave me my copy of the ten-year iron-clad guarantee from his parent company. "If anything goes wrong," he said, "remember that this company is as solid as Gibraltar. Make air-raid shelters for the government, you know." We thanked him and said good-bye.

In March, before we had had our first proper swim in the pool, I got a phone call from Vito. He hemmed and hawed and he sounded distressed, so I said quietly, "Your solid-as-Gibraltar parent pool company has gone bankrupt."

"Yes," he said. "How did you know?"

"I guessed," I said.

"I just want you to know," he said, "that I'll personally make good anything that goes wrong. Nothing extra."

I was touched and said, "Thank you, Vito." Then, after a pause, "Just tell me one thing. Did they go bankrupt with the swimming pools?"

"No," he said, "they got caught in a government scandal. They went bankrupt with the air-raid shelters."

Muriel had been out. When she got home I told her. She shuddered. "I'm wondering, darling," she said, "if maybe we're getting in a little over our heads."

chapter ix

Our first winter on Titicus Mountain was quite an experience. Shortly after the swimming pool was completed, the snow swirled down the mountain from the northeast and in about twenty-four hours, the frozen pool—along with everything else—was under a heavy eight-inch blanket of white. The blanket, augmented by fresh snow every few days, remained until late in March. It was a source of great frustration. People would visit us at the house and we'd want to show off the pool and they'd look at the flat expanse of white and say, *"What* pool?" I'd say, feebly, "It's under there." Most of them probably believed me, but by now I'd developed a complex about my invisible asset and I'd throw my back out digging down through the snow to prove, at least, that there was ice underneath. I couldn't get through the ice. By Christmas time it was about three feet thick and unassailable.

The temperatures on the mountain frequently were anywhere from fifteen degrees above zero to ten below. It didn't take us long to realize we were living in our own private Antarctica. We'd drive the seven miles, all downhill, to "downstreet," the city of Danbury, and downstreet would be ten degrees warmer. If we went farther downstreet to New York City, some sixty-five miles away, there would be a fifteen-to-twenty-degree difference. Often, as we drove up from downstreet, we'd be in a steady downpour of rain until we started to climb the mountain. Then it would be blizzard. After paying twenty dollars per blizzard to have our driveway plowed out I got an idea—following the third plowing.

I went to Steave and I said, "Isn't there some kind of snow-blowing attachment you can use on your tractor?"

His eyes grew dreamy. "Yes, sir," he said. "Every year I go to the Danbury Fair and I look at that beauty which is made for my machine."

"How much is it?" I asked.

"Oh, about a hundred and fifty dollars."

I did a quick mental calculation, based on the twenty dollars per plowing I was now paying. "Tell you what I'm gonna do," I said to Steave. *"I'll* buy the snow blower and *you* plow out my driveway every time it snows—for life."

Steave beamed happily and I bought the snow blower. Thereafter, whenever it snowed, I could hear him chugging methodically away in my driveway before he went to work in the morning. After the sixth blizzard, he came into the house for his customary cup of coffee. He looked at me with narrowed eyes, and said, "You know, I think I got took on this deal. How did you get to be a Yankee so fast?"

This was the *only* area in which any of us exhibited any Yankee cunning in the traditional battle with the rugged New England winter. Carol, for example, came home from school one weekend with a bevy of class-mates and a toboggan, mounted rakishly on the sloping back of a Volkswagen. Their plan for the weekend was to toboggan down the mountain on the road through the woods made by Vito and his brothers as their truck hauled earth from the pool excavation up to the nether end of the property. I joined Carol at the banked run she and her friends had constructed and I said, "What happens at the bottom? There's Newton's Law of Grav-ity, you know." One of Carol's male friends, a physics major, looked at me condescendingly. "Oh, don't worry, sir," he said. "I've got it figured out on solid engineering principles. We bank around this turn on the bottom and then head uphill again until we stop."

"If you say so," I replied, and I sat down on the knee of a snowman to watch.

The first run down the mountain was a beauty. Carol and four friends huddled together on the toboggan, with the physics major at the controls, and they zoomed down the run at about sixty miles an hour. At the bottom, the toboggan burst right through the snowbank, continued through a hemlock hedge, sailed over the six-foot-high wall that borders our property on Connecticut Route 39, and after orbiting in space for another twenty-five feet, landed upside down in the four-foot-deep snow. After ascertaining that no one had been hurt, I became aware of a strange presence in a gray uniform and a wide-brimmed hat. It was Oscar Lopes, our friendly neighborhood Connecticut State Policeman.

"What the *hell* are you doing with that thing flying over a state highway?" Oscar sputtered.

"I'm not doing *anything* with it, Oscar," I said. "Carol has a friend here who has it all figured out on solid engineering principles."

Oscar turned to Carol. "Do you realize you nearly hit the roof of my car with that damned thing?" he said.

"I'm sorry, Oscar," said Carol, showing all her dimples.

By now Oscar was visibly calming down. He thumbed through a well-worn book he pulled out of his pocket. "I don't see any law about flying over a public highway in a toboggan," he said after a while. Putting the book away, he glowered at the physics major. "I don't know what college you go to, Sonny," he said, "but you ain't ready to graduate." He stomped off to his car. The physics major and I then stomped off to the bottom of the toboggan run, where Steave was now watching the proceedings with considerable amusement. Using Steave's solid engineering principles, we then constructed a huge wall of snow to brake the toboggan's descent at the bottom of the hill. The physics major slunk into the house to listen to his record collection, which consisted of nothing but drums and other percussion instruments.

Carol and her friends came and went throughout the winter, each time discovering new means of sliding down the mountain. Muriel and I didn't have to; we had our own patented method. At least once a day, one of us would be outside and our feet would go out from under us and we would move along for a few feet on the derriere. This was because we were now on an economy kick (the building of the pool had nearly broken us) and Muriel's budget would not allow for the purchase of suitable winter boots. We finally solved the problem by my digging out my old paratrooper boots from my Army days, and Muriel buying a pair of rubber-soled workman's shoes at J. C. Penney for about $4.95. We looked pretty ludicrous but at least we were able to remain vertical.

The most ludicrous-looking one of us all was Naomi, who was born and raised in tropical climes and had never before had to face sub-zero weather and deep snow. She only emerged from the house twice a day to dump the garbage about a hundred feet away and she prepared for each excursion into the outdoors like a soldier in Washington's army going out to stand guard duty at Valley Forge. She wore two overcoats, galoshes, three scarves and homemade leggings of flannel rags with which she encased her legs from ankle to thigh. Naomi muttered constantly about the cold and even though we had purchased an electric blanket for her room, she ostentatiously journeyed to New York and bought another. She slept *between* the two electric blankets. Only when she was tucked away in her electrified sack was she happy, referring to herself philosophically as "the world's biggest hamburger between two toasted buns."

Despite her aversion to the snow, Naomi, a gracious hostess, would not hesitate to brave it if such action would bring pleasure to one of our occasional house guests. Once, we had as a weekend visitor a young man named Robert Wool, who was editor of a magazine to which I contributed. Wool, a Dartmouth graduate, arrived with ice skates and a hockey stick with which he had been proficient in his college days, and he spent all of one morning looking longingly at the frozen pond across the road. The only trouble was that there was about two feet of snow on the pond. Muriel and I had to leave for a couple of hours and when we got back, there was Wool skating happily on the pond and flailing away at some impromptu puck with his hockey stick. From the house, however, it seemed that he was surrounded by snow and as he sped along he was only visible from the waist up. Naomi noticed our puzzlement and hastened to explain. "Mr. Bob went out there and started to shovel," she said, "and I went out and said I would help him. Then I figured out we'd never be able to shovel a whole square, like he wanted, and I said, 'Why don't we make it like a racetrack and leave the snow in the middle?' " She chuckled. "Look at that little rascal," she said. "He looks like the rabbit at the dog track." And so he did—especially since he was soon pursued on his oval ice path by every stray dog and kid in the neighborhood.

Aside from extraordinary expenditures for liniment for guests like Wool plus one hundred dollars' worth of masonry work on our fireplace, which filled the house with smoke the first time we lighted a fire in it, we got through most of the winter without another financial disaster. Then, one day in February, Muriel and I had to make a quick trip to California. We got back to the house, after having been away less than a week, and as I opened the back door, an ovenlike blast of heat rushed out to meet us. "You can't beat these heating systems in these old houses," I said proudly.

"You sure can't," said Muriel, and she began to weep.

"What's the matter?" I asked.

"Look at our plants," she wailed. "All dead. All burned up."

I looked, and sure enough, every house plant had withered away into a brown crisp. Muriel wailed again. "And the candles. Where *are* they?"

"There they are," I said. "They are pools of wax all over the tables."

"Wah-ah-ah," said Muriel.

"I'd better call Steave," I said.

Steave came over, took one look and immediately plunged down into the cellar. I followed him and watched as he examined the furnace, all the time whistling nervously to himself. Finally he said, "You had a close call here, kiddo."

"Oh," I said offhandedly. "What's a little wax on the tables?"

"Kiddo," he said, "this furnace ran away. Something

went wrong with the controls and it must of kept going without turning off for three days straight. I bet the temperature up there in the house was over two hundred degrees. The only thing that kept the house from burning down was them old beams, which are like rock after all these years. Even so, they would have gone if the steam didn't escape and short-circuit these wires here when the boiler cracked."

My offhand manner abruptly disappeared. "When the boiler *what?*" I asked.

"Cracked," Steave said.

"How much?" I asked.

"About three hundred dollars' worth," he said.

"Wah-ah-ah," I said.

I dragged myself upstairs and phoned the men who would come to do the three hundred dollars' worth on the furnace. Steave went home and I slumped weakly in a chair. I could hear Muriel wailing off in remote parts of the house as she discovered new wax damage. "You and your candles," I yelled. "Who do you think you are, a goddam Mme. Tussaud?" Muriel came downstairs and hit me.

She then disappeared into the linen closet and emerged with a sheet onto which had melted all the Christmas candles she had stored on the top shelf. "Wait a minute," I said, "that's a very interesting pattern." She prepared to hit me again, but I said, "No, I mean it. Look at that part of the sheet with the reds and yellows and greens. Looks just like a Jackson Pollock." Muriel halted in mid-assault and stared at the sheet. "You're right," she said, "and that part up the left-hand corner. A Brown-period Braque if I ever saw one." We spent the next hour studying the wax-encrusted sheet and we discovered sections that looked like Pereira, Picasso and even Georgia O'Keeffe paintings. It helped break the tension.

About a week later, I noticed Muriel working on the sheet with a pair of scissors. She cut out the Pollock, the Braque and Picasso, and the next thing I knew she had taken them downstreet and had them framed. When they got back from the framers, there was a little signature in black wax in the corner of each. The signature read "Castelucci."

"Who the hell is Castelucci?" I asked.

"The guy who was supposed to check our furnace and didn't and the wax melted on the sheet," said Muriel.

"What are you up to?" I asked suspiciously.

"You'll see," she said.

The following week there was a native handicrafts show at the King Street Firehouse and two of the Casteluccis sold for thirty dollars apiece. Muriel had a little table at the show and she gave an exhibition to the ladies on the new art form of painting on linen with melted wax.

About a month later, we had a party at the house for some of our city friends. One of the guests was a movie director we knew who was visiting from Hollywood. The director left early and when he nervously said good-bye to me he had a package under his arm that was approximately the same size as our remaining Castelucci, the Picasso.

I sought Muriel out and with a significant glance at the retreating back of the movie director, I asked, "Castelucci?"

"Uh-huh," she said, smiling at one of the passing ladies.

"How *could* you?" I said.

"Oh, he just *had* to have it," she said, "and I told him I'd give it to him on one condition—that we keep it a secret from you, because you love it so. He's supposed to be your friend, but he didn't bat an eye at betraying you. He even insisted on paying for it."

"How much?" I said.

"Oh, about three hundred dollars' worth," Muriel said. And she moved off graciously to join a discussion of our State Department's policy in Vietnam.

chapter x

A few days after the sale of the last of the Caste-luccis, Muriel and I were trudging through the snow outside the house when suddenly she stopped and studied the Braeburn Inn sign. I paid no attention because I had been too lazy to lace up my paratrooper boots that morning and I was busy trying to keep loose snow from getting into the flapping tops of the boots. Muriel said, "We got the house to go with the sign, and now I think we ought to get a dog to go with the house."

I came to such an abrupt stop that about a half bushel of snow got into my boots. "How's that again?" I asked.

"A dog," she said. "A nice big dog whom I can love and cherish."

"But you've got *me* to love and cherish," I said.

"That's not enough," she said. "I want someone who won't talk back and who won't demean me when I say something stupid."

"I haven't demeaned you in three days," I said. "Besides, dogs talk back. They bark. Also, sometimes they demean you by biting."

This didn't work, so I tried another approach.

"How about our budget?" I said. "The kind of dog you're talking about that doesn't talk back or demean costs a lot of money."

"Well," Muriel said, "there's my profit from the sale of the Casteluccis."

"What do you mean, *profit?*" I said. "You made three hundred and sixty dollars and it cost just about that to repair the damage from the furnace. Just when we're becoming cunning Yankees instead of city bumpkins you want to spoil it all."

"Oh, no," she said with cunning Yankee logic. "I know that the insurance company paid for fixing the furnace. If we shop for Henry carefully with our Yankee cunning, we can still come out with a pretty good profit."

"Who's Henry?" I asked.

"Henry's the name of the dog we're going to buy," she said.

I knew I was defeated, so we went into the house to discuss what type of dog Henry was going to be.

The first suggestion came from Naomi. She launched into a long diatribe on the virtues of the Chihuahua, which, I was fascinated to learn, was native to her Panama as well as to Mexico. We listened to a stirring account, which Naomi acted out with gestures, about how a heroic Chihuahua named Pedro had aroused the Presidential Palace in Panama City and had saved Presidente Roberto Chiari from being overthrown in a midnight coup. Naomi's description of the abortive revolt was more exciting than anything we had seen on television in weeks, but when she was finished I said, "Chiari *deserved* to be overthrown. Besides, we want a big dog. A Chihuahua only weighs about two pounds."

"Then get a *big* Chihuahua," roared Naomi, waving her arms.

"No," said Muriel. "Besides, who ever heard of a Chihuahua named Henry?"

"Then call him Enrique," reasoned Naomi, but knowing she had lost, she retired to the basement to finish her laundry.

The next breed to be championed was the Great Dane, by, of course, Carol. We always knew that one of Carol's major ambitions was to be able to walk down Fifth Avenue in New York with either a Great Dane or a leopard on a leash, but she had sense enough not to bespeak this resolve. Instead she said, "A Dane could pull the toboggan up the hill and protect Mother when she's alone in the house, and all like that."

"Too big," I said. "He wouldn't fit in the car and I'm not going to buy a new car to go with the new dog." Carol subsided and Muriel suggested a poodle. I answered, with sweet reasonableness, "I wouldn't be caught dead walking a poodle." We all lapsed into thought and then Muriel said, "What's that great shaggy beast with the hair in its eyes that we see in TV commercials all the time?"

"Ah," I said, "the Old English Sheepdog, a noble creature."

"How do you know?" asked Carol.

"You wouldn't understand the meaning of the term," I said, "but I was poor when I was a boy. I was working my way through college, and the best friend I had was an Old English Sheepdog, name of Digby."

"Oh, *that* old story," said Carol.

"Don't interrupt your father, dear, when he's telling his anecdotes," said Muriel. "Besides, I don't think we ever heard the part about the dog before."

Undaunted, I pressed ahead. I said, "Unlike some other people I know whose fathers pay for everything while they are in college, I had to work for my athletic scholarship in track and work during the football season building bleachers and handing out towels to the football players—"

"And collecting their dirty sweat socks after practice," interrupted Carol.

"Right," I said. "And at night I'd work in the kitchen of my fraternity house and wait on tables for my meals."

"And the only reason they pledged you to the fraternity was because your uncle was the national president and they had to," interrupted Carol.

"Right," I said.

"But where does the dog come in?" asked Muriel.

"Well," I said, "every night after I finished my work in the kitchen and had done my studying, all the other guys in the fraternity would be talking about where they were going with their dates the next weekend and how much money they were going to spend, and they would plan to go downtown to see Benny Goodman and things like that. I would feel very lonely then because I didn't even have enough money for subway fare and would go outside by myself and there would be Digby waiting for me."

"What was an Old English Sheepdog doing out there in the middle of the night?" asked Carol in a small voice. Her manner was subdued, however, and a tear was beginning to form in the corner of her left eye.

"Digby," I said, "belonged to the fraternity house next door. The guys in *that* house were even richer and snobbier than my own brothers. But Digby didn't know about things like that and he loved me. Whenever he saw me, he'd put his front paws on my shoulders and kiss me all over the face, and then we'd wrestle and he'd help me practice my sprint starts, and we'd play a little catch with an old tennis ball I kept in my room. I think Digby loved me and I loved him because we were the only poor kids on the block and he recognized that and we had a real community of interest. The only allowance *he* got was two bones a week, and if I asked him, he would even share that with me."

By now, both Muriel and Carol were weeping openly. "That settles it," Muriel sobbed. "Henry *has* to be an Old English Sheepdog."

The first time we laid eyes on Henry was about three weeks later in Hingham, Massachusetts. The reason Henry was in Hingham, Massachusetts, is that he had just been born there, in the home of a lady named Laura Fegan. The reason *we* were in Hingham, Massachusetts, which is near Boston and about one hundred and fifty miles from our home, is that we had started to shop around for an Old English Sheepdog with Yankee cunning and had discovered that there wasn't much of a market in which to do so, Laura Fegan, in fact, being the *only* market. There wasn't another breeder in the entire United States who had a litter at that particular time.

So there we were, looking at Henry, and he was looking at us through beady little black eyes which had just opened because he was only two weeks old. We identified him as Henry by the white dewlap on his black ear, a marking which none of his eight brothers and sisters had. Henry was a three-pound black-and-white blob barely able to drag himself around on the floor. I was impressed when he took an immediate interest in my right shoe, which he proceeded to bite, but I whispered to Muriel, "Are you sure he's an Old English Sheepdog? He looks like a skunk." Muriel didn't answer, but she looked worried.

Just then we heard a disturbance at the front door of Miss Fegan's house. She opened the door and in loped two huge, shaggy creatures, whom Miss Fegan introduced as Henry's mother, Suzie, and his grandmother, Mittens. Suzie immediately occupied herself with her young, but Mittens, a magnificent gray-and-white animal weighing perhaps a hundred pounds, leaped gleefully at me. Rearing up on her hind legs to her full standing height of five feet six inches, she placed a great hairy paw on each of my shoulders and began mopping my face with her immense pink tongue. I wrestled with Mittens for a while, as I had once done with Digby, and I said happily to Muriel, "There's nothing to worry about, dear. If this is his grandma, Henry's an Old English Sheepdog, all right."

After confirming this more or less emotional verdict with a more scientific check on Henry's pedigree papers, we paid Miss Fegan a deposit and arranged to return to fetch him when he was old enough to leave home. That would be eight weeks later. During the waiting period, we'd ask each other questions like, "When's that hairy chap coming to live with us?" Finally the day arrived, but Muriel was sick in bed, so Carol and I drove up to get the new addition to the family. By now, Henry had grown a foot in height and fifteen pounds in weight and he was covered from nose to rear (he had no tail) with the long silky hair that is typical of his breed. Laura Fegan said, "I've taught him his name. Call him."

I said, "Come here, Henry." His enormous floppy ears went up and he came staggering over to me, baby-like, nipping, at the same time, at the flank of one of his sisters. He tried to reach up to my shoulders, as his grandmother had done, but even though I was kneeling, he couldn't quite make it. He wept and I lowered my face nearly to the floor. He seized my face with both paws and the mopping routine began. "Daddy," said Carol, "you are hooked."

On the way home, I nearly got *unhooked*. We placed Henry between us on the front seat of the car, and the minute he became aware that he had been taken away from his mother and grandmother, he started making the strangest noise either Carol or I had ever heard. It was a combination of the loud bleat of a lamb and the cry of the South American puma. There was absolutely nothing even remotely canine about the sound. After about a half hour of this ear-splitting wail, I turned to Carol and said, "My God, do you think we have to go through life listening to *that?*" Carol's reply was a look of sheer despair. By the time we reached Worcester, Massachusetts, however, Henry had ceased his protest, and was standing with his paws on the back seat, watching the passing traffic with total amazement. At the toll booth near the Connecticut border, he reached over and kissed the hand of the toll taker. From Hartford to Danbury, he slept peacefully with his head on my lap. When we arrived home, he relieved himself on the front lawn and moved in as if he had lived there all his life.

Since we pride ourselves in being an educated family, Muriel almost immediately arranged for the schooling of the new addition to the clan. It gave us a wrench to do so, but for his own good Henry was sent to board at the Ruth Roberts Obedience Training School for Dogs. He took his instruction there from Miss Roberts,

Mondays through Fridays. On Saturdays and Sundays he came home to live with us and unlearned all the knowledge he had assimilated during the week. After about three weeks of this schizophrenic existence, Henry became a dropout, planting all four feet firmly on the ground and with all the obstinacy a four-month-old could muster, refusing to go back to school. Although we lamented his decision, we decided to go along with it because he had at least mastered the fundamentals. His latrine habits were orderly, he could walk on a leash, he obeyed simple commands such as "Stay" and "Come," and, all in all, his IQ seemed sufficiently high to enable him to continue his education privately at home.

His education was sometimes on the unorthodox side. I would sit him down in front of me and he would listen patiently as I told him over and over again, "You are a dog. I am a man." Then for the benefit of Naomi, who frequently lapsed into Spanish, I'd translate into that language: *"Yo soy hombre. Usted es perro."* The idea of this was to familiarize Henry with the idea that I was the boss, but I gave up this approach after Steave eavesdropped on the lesson one day and walked away shaking his head in disbelief.

Henry also learned something about the physical states of matter through direct scientific experimentation. When he first arrived, the swimming pool, of course, was frozen with a heavy layer of snow on it. He frolicked on the surface the same as he did on any other surface. One week there was a thaw, however. Henry and Muriel had been in New York together while I was away in California, and one night, after performing on a television panel show, Muriel decided to return to the country. She and Henry went up to inspect the premises and Henry started to cut across the pool, as usual. The next thing Muriel knew, Henry was floundering in the water in the deep end and she was drenched, from the bottom of her new gown to the top of her new coiffure, trying to pull him out. By that time, Henry was quite bulky, weighing about seventy pounds dripping wet, but Muriel managed to rescue him by yanking on his beard at one end and on the three-inch fur of his rump on the other end. It took six Turkish towels and thirty-six hours to dry him out.

Henry apparently was a slow learner in elementary physics. A few days later, Naomi came out of the house with his bowl full of drinking water. Thinking the bowl contained food, Henry, remembering what I had taught him about the shortest distance between two points being a straight line, once again tried to run across the unfrozen surface of the pool. This time he landed in the shallow end and there he stood, with his back feet on the bottom and his front feet clutching the coping around the edge of the pool. He looked at me and hollered. I yanked him out and dried him off, and this time the lesson took. He never went into the pool again. In fact, it became a hazard for *anyone* to use the pool after that. Apparently remembering his own unpleasant experiences, he sets up an anguished howl of concern and runs frenziedly around the pool barking furious warnings every time someone goes in for a swim.

Henry learned pretty fast that when you've got long hair you don't go into burr patches in the woods and that a raccoon is not just another little dog to play with. He was slow, however, in acquiring watchdog aptitudes. When a stranger came to the house, Henry would bellow with glee and leap upon the man in an attempt to kiss him on the face. We finally convinced him that he should change the bellow to lower, more ominous tones. But he never could learn to give up his kissing habit. Muriel solved the problem by not allowing Henry to approach strangers and by relying on the sound alone to frighten off potential footpads. She'd hold our straining beast by the collar and mention how vicious he was. The strangers, not knowing for what purpose Henry was *really* trying to get at them, invariably would back off.

At night, however, Henry was totally unreliable.

He'd go to sleep when we did (usually on the floor at the foot of our bed, although he had the entire house in which to slumber) and when he slept he was out for the night. He wouldn't rouse himself until one of us got up in the morning, and even then, he was like a half-awake man who hadn't yet had his coffee. One night, Muriel was alone in the house with our four-footed guardian, when she heard a strange noise in the living room. She said, "Henry, get up." Henry raised his head slightly, grunted, and then went right back to sleep. After two more attempts to rouse him, Muriel armed herself with a fireplace poker and slipped out into the living room. She saw a sinister movement near the front door and shrank back in terror. Finally, as her eyes became accustomed to the predawn half-light in the living room, she realized what it was. Both the noise and movement were being made by the wind whipping through an open window against a drape. She closed the window and crept back to bed. Henry was still snoozing peacefully away. Fortunately, his job aptitude in that particular area improved as he grew out of adolescence.

Henry did do well in certain other subjects. He was excellent at herding, for example. Not having any sheep or cattle to herd, he sharpened his talents on small children who occasionally visited the house. When the children were playing outside, he'd keep them all in a neat little group, and if a moppet strayed, Henry would leap into action and push the child back into the main herd with gentle nudges of his big hairy head.

He also did well at learning simple canine tricks, such as shaking hands. He performed this feat desultorily for a while, not quite understanding its pragmatic value. He learned, however, on his first New Year's Eve. At midnight, we all drank champagne and, in traditional manner, kissed each other. Henry watched this ritual for a moment. Then he lapped up some champagne from a glass left carelessly on a coffee table. After that he solemnly walked around and shook hands with everybody.

chapter xi

It was a late spring that year. The crocuses, in fact, bloomed through a thin layer of snow and the sound of the cricket was not yet heard in the land. One day near the end of April, Henry heard a strange noise emanating from the Bjelko house, more than a quarter of a mile away, and took off through the woods to play with his friend, Chipper, the Bjelko's new Dalmatian (their first Dalmatian, Boots, had died the previous autumn). When I caught up with Henry to drag him back home, I came upon Steave cutting up firewood with a chain saw. Steave, who liked to take advantage of my still considerable ignorance, noticed my inquiring look and commented, "Still about six weeks of winter to go, up here on the mountain." I believed him and carried this intelligence back to Muriel, who said, "Oh, no!" and lapsed into a deep depression. That very afternoon the temperature went up to eighty and stayed there.

The next few weeks were a period of intense discovery for all of us. Not knowing what the previous owner had planted, we prowled the estate looking excitedly to see what was popping out of the ground. Steave acquainted us with daffodils, tulips and hyacinth. The peonies emerged like red worms and Muriel didn't believe Steave when he identified them as flowers, preferring to avoid that part of the side lawn until the "worms" began to sprout shoots of green. Henry, too, was in a new world of discovery. A tame robin named Irving, whom we had befriended the summer before, returned to the area and took to eating the marrow out of Henry's bones in his yard. Henry was driven to distraction by this lack of manners and chased Irving futilely, to the point of his own exhaustion. Finally, he'd lie in his yard in resignation, watching Irving eat his bone just a foot or so from his head. Then he'd growl and make an exasperated rush at Irving, who would merely fly gracefully up onto the fence and then return. Henry also had a difficult time with the moles, another new creature in his life. He'd hear a mole wending its way under the turf. He'd put his massive hair-covered head to the ground and follow the progress of the mole all over the lawn. Crouched down and with no tail or visible eyes, he once startled a half-tanked bum passing on the road. The bum said to me, "Man, that's the biggest caterpillar I've ever seen."

As such things happen in a small town, Henry by now

was famous in the area. I'd take him with me to a shopping center and total strangers would walk up and say, "Hello, Henry." Parents would drive by the property with their children in their car to greet Henry where he sat regally in his fenced-in yard. Once I ordered a new refrigerator at Sears, Roebuck and I had to explain to the salesman where the house was, so the delivery could be made. The salesman said, "Oh, that's the old red clapboard where Henry lives."

As he grew out of his adolescence, Henry became a massive 110-pounder, who, when we wrestled, usually could throw me two falls out of three. Despite his size, he could run like a cheetah and proved to be quite a distraction to Aaron, Janie's young nephew, whom we had engaged to help take care of the grounds after I had nearly burned down the mountain. Aaron was a compactly built, muscular twenty-two-year-old just out of the Navy, and sensing that he was a better physical match for him than I was, Henry would hurl himself at Aaron, seeking friendly combat, every time the youth was stooped over tending to his gardening duties.

There were other distractions for Aaron. I had set up a ping-pong table near the pool, and when he finished his work, I'd play five or six games with him. After that, Aaron would refresh himself with a swim in the pool. Then, Muriel would usually ask him to come into the house for a cup of coffee. He'd sit for a while and we'd discuss the news events of the day. He'd question me closely on such matters as how Congress worked and what were the psychological motivations behind a man like Frank Sinatra. One day Muriel said, "You and your big mouth. We're going to lose a perfectly good gardener."

"What do you mean?" I asked.

"You'll see," she said darkly, and terminated the conversation.

Surely enough, at the end of April Aaron came to me and said, "Mr. Davidson, I'm sorry to have to tell you this, but I won't be able to work for you any more."

Muriel looked smug. "Why?" I asked.

"Well," said Aaron, "sittin' around and talkin' to you onto it and all, I decided I don't want to be ignorant. I'm goin' back to high school to get my diploma and then I want to go on to college."

Stunned, I bid Aaron Godspeed. Muriel wished him well, too. I went outside and snapped a spade handle trying to plant a juniper in the rocky soil.

The next few weeks were a period of severe regression for us. With Aaron gone and Steave engrossed in his Zoning Board and firehouse meetings, Muriel began to read the mail-order seed and nursery catalogues again—and all of our new-found Yankee cunning departed us. Muriel read: " 'Yours! A bonanza of Western beauty. . . . From the sky-reaching mountains of the far West comes one of the most exciting trees in years. . . . When you see these young giants, you'll recognize how different they are from most evergreens. . . . Within the year they'll zoom another full foot or two, look so authentic you'll expect to find the sheriff's posse camping beneath them. . . .' " Along with this breathtaking copy was a photograph of a magnificent pine tree reaching up to the sky with its seven-inch-long needles.

"Great," I said. "Let's order six of those young giants and we'll line the driveway with them."

We sent away for the young giants and a week later they arrived from upstate New York. We didn't know they had arrived for several hours because they were resting quietly in a foot-long package in our mailbox and we hadn't been home when the RFD postman passed by. I opened the box and there were six scraggly twigs, scarcely bigger in overall dimension than the seven-inch needles promised by the catalogue. As I stood at the mailbox staring at the twigs, Steave came down the road on his tractor. He paused and glanced at my bonanza of Western beauty. "What's that?" he asked. "Whisk brooms?"

"No," I said. "These are young giants."

"What are they supposed to do?" he asked.

"They are supposed to zoom a full foot or two within the year," I replied, "and look so authentic you'll expect to find the sheriff's posse camping beneath them."

Steave started his tractor and made ready to move on. "About the only posse small enough to fit under them young giants," he said, "is ants."

"How long would it take," I asked, "for these young giants to grow up to be big enough for folks to camp under them?

"About fifty years," said Steave, chugging off.

"Oh," I said. "I wonder why they didn't mention that in the catalogue."

Muriel at least was able to make some use of the young giants as a table decoration, beefed up with irises. She was not as fortunate, however, with some other items that caught her eye in the catalogues. There was, for example, "the Living Fence, a beautiful thick hedge in six weeks, bursting with roses all summer, with berries all winter, and strong enough so that even a bull can't crash through it." The Living Fence, when it arrived, consisted of seventy-five eight-inch-long cuttings of the common multiflora rose, which grows almost like a weed in Connecticut. Muriel steadfastly planted them, nevertheless. In six weeks, the eight-inch cuttings had grown up to be nine-inch cuttings. Not owning a bull, we then decided to test our Living Fence by having Henry try to crash through it. Since he could easily walk *over* the "impenetrable barrier," as it had been advertised, we had considerable trouble getting him to assay a crash. When he did, the impenetrable barrier tangled itself in his hair and he simply walked away with most of the Living Fence torn out by the roots and dangling from his coat.

Then there was the Fountain Tree Rose, which, the catalogue promised, would "start blooming this very spring and provide graceful cascades of red roses all season long." For ten dollars, exhorted the catalogue, "you can watch the amazed glances of your neighbors when they burst into bloom." This particular phrase caused Muriel to pause in the reading of the catalogue. "That's interesting," she said. "I can't wait to see some of our neighbors burst into bloom." She read on: "Plant the Fountain Tree in front of a picture window and enjoy the loveliness of hundreds of dazzling big Roses indoors and outside! So hardy and vigorous they laugh at conditions that would kill their weaker cousins!"

So Muriel invested ten dollars in a Fountain Tree Rose and planted it outside the closest thing we had to a picture window—the downstairs bathroom casement. It looked like a cane with a clump of roots growing from its top. We waited for the cascade of ever-blooming rose glory, but the Fountain Tree remained the same Medusa-topped walking stick. Guests would pause in our bathroom and remark, "What an interesting driftwood sculpture." By late June, only a few leaves had sprung from the Fountain Tree's topknot and Steave suggested that maybe we had planted it upside down. He examined it and, "No, I guess you put it in right."

"What do you suggest?" asked Muriel with quavering underlip.

"I suggest," he said, "that you burn all them catalogues and that I find you another gardener."

That's how Adam came into our lives.

chapter xii

A dam (his real name is Ray Adams but nobody ever calls him that, except maybe the Government) turned out to be a sandy-haired Yankee of about fifty-five with the weatherbeaten face of a farmer in a Grant Wood painting and the stooped, muscular body of a blacksmith in an Early American movie about the Devil and Daniel Webster. Neither of these characteristics was surprising, since he had been born and raised on a farm just down the road and he plied the well-digger's trade, lifting and emplacing enormous bits and drills with the great strength he had developed in his back and arms.

When he first arrived and began restoring order to our mishandled acres, Adam was taciturn to the point of nearly total silence, and Muriel observed, "we're not going to lose *this* one to the Halls of Ivy." But then as I began to amuse him with my bumbling but good-natured attempts at assistance, he gradually opened up with occasional conversation. At first he dealt mostly in tragedy. He'd say, "Did you hear about the car that ran off the road and hit the stone wall down at the Sonneborn place?" and proceed to tell me all the gory details he had witnessed while helping to pull victims out of the wreckage.

Later, he began to fill me in on his own close calls with death. On one occasion, apparently, he was clearing a pile of brush and realized he had picked up a five-foot copperhead along with some dead branches. He said, "I looked that snake right in the eye and I hypmotized it, saying over and over again, 'Swush, swush, get back in the brush.' Then that snake put his head down and I threw the snake and the branches away from me as far as I could, and I run away in the other direction. I looked back and that snake was still layin' there, still hypmotized."

Another time, Adam came to work immediately after a particularly violent thunderstorm. "Well," he said cheerfully, "I nearly met my Maker today."

"Oh?" I said.

"Yep," he said. "Was workin' on a well over there in Germantown and this big storm cloud come up and I wanted to get the bit out of the well before it commenced rainin'. I'm standin' on the metal plate, holdin' the bit in my arms, when there's this big flash of lightnin'. It hits the top of the bit and it sounds like a bomb went off. The bit turns red and sparks jump out from all over it and then all of that electricity goes through me. I fall to the ground and my whole body turns black. The next thing I know the other fellers are clustered around me on the ground and they're sayin', 'Adam, we thought sure you was dead. Your whole body turned black and you was unconscious for ten minutes.' I get to my feet then and I see that the only thing that saved me was that I'm wearin' rubber-soled shoes. The rubber is smokin' and I smell just like a car with burnin' brakes."

"How do you feel now?" I asked.

"Well," he said, "it still smarts a bit but I guess I'm OK." He then turned away from me and devoted himself to wrestling a two-hundred-pound boulder out of the hillside.

Adam was the natural-born enemy of the thrip, the lace bug and the caterpillar. Moles, when they heard his footfall, would flee across the boundary to the next property. On the other hand, he was a sort of St. Francis when it came to the local bird life. He'd bring mysterious bird-food concoctions which he mixed up at home, and the area swarmed with cardinals, varicolored finches and other exotic feathered creatures we had never seen before. Once I noticed a bright-blue and a yellow-green pair feeding among the rest. "What kind of birds are those?" I asked.

Adam replied, "Oh, them's a couple of parakeets escaped from the Vincents' downstreet. They foller me around on the job."

Adam also was a genius about poking around in the

woods and finding items to transplant on the lawns near the house. He'd discover mountain laurel, for example, for which I had been paying four dollars per bush at the nursery. On one occasion he decided to chop down an old peach tree which had died and I suggested going to the nursery to buy a maple tree to replace it. He looked at me as if I was crazy. He pointed to the forest surrounding the house and said, "What do you think them are in the woods? Maple. Hundreds of 'em. Now you can go down there to the nursery and pay twenty-five dollars for a ten-foot maple if you want, but *you* got maple in your woods worth maybe a hunnert dollars apiece to that nursery feller." I slunk away into the woods with Adam and selected a magnificent young maple for transplanting in the fall. Adam looked at me disgustedly. "You're like the starvin' Indian," he said, "livin' on top of a oil field."

Adam was a total iconoclast, both in personal habit and in outlook. He eschewed the dress normally worn by local laborers (overalls, pronounced "over-hauls") and showed up for work wearing a baseball cap, a Hawaiian-print sport shirt and slacks. He habitually had a large, usually unlighted Italian cigar shoved into the corner of his mouth. Politically, without realizing it, he was close to being an anarchist. He classified practically all local politicians of both parties as crooks and at elections he would write in such names as Donald Duck and Elizabeth Taylor for offices like mayor or councilman. The only officeholder for whom he had any use was Steave, whom he respectfully called The

President. Once, when I was backing young Abe Najamy (the MC at the Arab beauty contest) for Mayor of Danbury, Adam spat and muttered, "Them bums on the Town Committee won't give that boy the nomination. They want someone they can control so they can keep on fillin' their pockets." A week later, Najamy was passed over for Mayor and had to run for City Treasurer instead.

Despite the fact, however, that Adam considered my knowledge of local politics to be on the same level of ignorance as my knowledge of local trees, he never failed to show up when I made a speech on some pressing local matter. Once, for example, I addressed a mass meeting in the gymnasium of the New Fairfield Junior High School on the need for new legislation to control teen-age drinking and driving. In the middle of my speech, I looked up and there was Adam sitting in the top row of the bleachers. When I finished, he stomped ostentatiously out of the room and would not tarry to listen to any of the other speakers.

Adam would show up at all hours of the day or night to tend our property. One evening at dusk I asked him why and he growled, "I seen this place here ever since the Wilkes family owned it when I was a boy and I ain't goin' to watch you let it go to pot." His fierce pride in the grounds was almost compulsive and he'd drive his friends around to see his handiwork. Occasionally, however, he expressed other motives for his dedication. One Sunday morning, I went out to the road to get the newspaper at about 7 A.M. and there was Adam feeding the hemlocks. "What *are* you doing here this early?" I asked.

"Oh," he said offhandedly, "I couldn't stand the arguin' at home so I come up here to work." He added, "There's no charge for today. I just want somethin' to do."

All in all, paying Adam became somewhat of a problem. He charged by the hour and he laboriously recorded the amount of time he worked in a little black book which he carried in his hip pocket. Every week we had a little ritual we went through. I'd press him to tell me the number of hours he had worked so I could write him a check, and invariably he'd mumble something about having left his little black book in his other pants. When I pursued the subject he'd finally come up with a figure which I *knew* was about half the number of hours he had actually worked.

I'd say, "You worked more than that, Adam. Why don't you look at your little black book again?"

He'd wet his thumb and studiously turn the pages in the book and he'd say, "Nope, that's right. Besides, if I charged you too much you might think I'm too expensive and not use me any more."

I'd say, "What kind of Yankee are *you?*"

He'd wink, thrust the little black book back into his pocket, and reply, "The smartest kind."

Adam had an impact on every member of the family. He indulged all of Carol's whimseys, helping her with any hobby which happened to be current in her ever-changing fancy—such as inundating her room with house plants or painting her furniture red. Carol had a habit, when she was low in spirit, of climbing to the roof of the garage and sitting there, next to the weather vane. She called this her brooding place, and she used it for introspective philosophizing much as Snoopy the dog uses the roof of his doghouse in the comic strip "Peanuts." After noting this phenomenon for several days, Adam climbed up onto the roof of the garage and installed a little foam-rubber upholstered seat to make Carol more comfortable in her brooding.

Adam and Naomi hit it off immediately. She called him "Oddum" and he called her "Nommy." She brought him cool tropical drinks to refresh him as he labored in the hot sun, and they would sit on one of the stone fences discussing such subjects as the proper place to plant corn and various disasters they had observed in their lives. I used to eavesdrop on these conversations and would marvel at how they managed to communicate with each other. Both were partially deaf; Adam's English was laconic and sprinkled with the local patois; Naomi, though bilingual, spoke the specialized Caribbean English of her Jamaican parents and frequently lapsed into long paragraphs of Spanish. Yet they gravely listened to each other with what was total understanding. Essentially they were both people of the soil, speaking an international language. The varying color of their skins seemed to make absolutely no difference to them.

In one of these conversations, Naomi told Adam about a friend of hers who had been eaten by a shark while swimming in the ocean near the Canal Zone in Panama. Adam countered with the story of a terrible disaster in Danbury years ago when a dam broke and drowned dozens of people. Naomi's rejoinder to this was a tale of voodoo ritualistic murder as witnessed by her mother in Jamaica in the 1890's. Adam, with nothing comparable in his repertoire, reached back for his best reserve story—the account of how he had turned black when struck by lightning, embellishing it with an anecdote about another well-digger in Brookfield who had indeed been incinerated by a bolt of lightning. After all this gore, they then politely discussed the best method of cross-pollinating beefsteak tomatoes. When they had settled this matter to their satisfaction, Naomi returned to her kitchen and Adam to his begonias.

The only one with whom Adam had any trouble was Henry. Our beast, who seemed to love everyone else in the world, took one look at Adam the first time he saw him and for some strange reason known only to himself, he backed away with a terrifying deep growl in his throat. Adam, an animal lover with several dogs of his own, was hurt by this strange reaction, but we explained it by saying Henry probably was just being loyal to Adam's predecessor, his pal Aaron. Adam accepted this explanation but Henry followed him around, sniffing suspiciously at his legs and emitting an occasional growl.

After that, Adam continued to try to make friends with Henry, but everything he did was wrong. He induced Henry to stand up and examine his face at close

hand to see how harmless he was, but he forgot to remove the cigar from his mouth and the stogie splat-
tered all over Henry's huge black nose. Henry backed
away and shook his head for hours trying to get rid of
the foul taste of fragments of cigar which had pene-
trated his lips.

Next, when Henry was away one afternoon, Adam
decided to surprise him by cleaning up his yard, which
was Henry's castle. Henry had carefully accumulated
every bone he had received since he had arrived during
the winter and he liked nothing better than to sit in his
yard surrounded by his bonanza of bones—a king of
the beasts in his own private jungle. The bones made
the yard look like a cemetery after an earthquake, but
Henry liked it so we had always left it the way it was.
Adam didn't know this, however, and he diligently
swept up all the bones and threw them away. When
Henry got home that afternoon, he rushed out into his
yard and immediately detected the loss. He sniffed
frantically in all the possible hiding places. Then, just
as realization dawned that the bones were indeed gone,
he spotted Adam burying the last of them up on the
hillside. He began to bark at Adam in a cavernous bass
that could be heard a half mile away. It was an unre-
stricted declaration of war.

After that, Henry wouldn't let Adam in the house
and he barked and growled at him whenever he saw
him outside. If he noted that Adam was digging up a
flower bed, he'd go over and relieve himself in it. Twice
I even caught him attempting to relieve himself on
Adam.

Finally, the situation got so bad that I decided I personally had to put a stop to it. I took Henry outside and brought him over to where Adam was working. Henry just sat there and watched sullenly. I stood right next to Adam and pumped his hand and put my arm around his shoulder. I said to Henry, "Now look. This man is a friend of mine. He's a friend of the whole family. I want you to act like a grown dog and not a child and come over here and make up with Adam."

Henry just sat there stubbornly and suspiciously and wouldn't move.

"Now come on," I urged.

Henry slowly pulled his great bulk to his feet and came walking over, shaking his head from side to side as if he were muttering to himself. He sat down in front of Adam and glowered at him for an instant. Then he put out his paw to shake hands and reared up to kiss Adam desultorily on the face.

After that, a general peace was restored. While he was not exactly friendly with Adam, Henry was at least civil.

chapter xiii

When the full heat of the summer descended on us, we began to wonder once again whether we had made a monstrous mistake. It wasn't the weather; it was the guests. With the swimming pool the undoubted principal attraction, we were swamped with unexpected visits from people we hadn't seen in years. At one point Muriel looked at the Braeburn Inn sign and commented, "Maybe we ought to change it to the Davidson Biltmore."

On weekends, particularly, I spent most of my time at the outdoor grill working nonstop at the preparation of hamburgers, hot dogs and other goodies. Muriel and Carol (who was now back from school for the summer) were the cocktail waitresses. Henry was the lifeguard at the pool.

The ping-pong table and the dart board were in constant use. Carol's college friends, mostly large, scholarly young men and angular girls with long, dank hair, frolicked in the pool all day and, under the lights, long after dark. Small boys climbed the apple and peach trees and pelted each other with the half-ripe fruit. The guests used gallons of suntan oil and the washing machine turned over two dozen clean towels a day. It got so bad that one Saturday afternoon, four total strangers showed up, disported themselves at the pool for several hours and then left. Everyone thought they had come with someone else.

One day, half of our silverware disappeared and Muriel said, "Aha! Now I *know* we're running a hotel." It turned out, however, that one of our lady guests, helping out with the cleanup after lunch, had absent-mindedly thrown the silver into the garbage with the paper plates. Fortunately, our garbage is collected only on Tuesdays and Saturdays so Henry and I were able to go through the slops and retrieve the silver.

That particular day was a classic. One of my male guests plunged into the pool and emerged snorting and snuffling. "You better watch it, feller," he said ominously.

I juggled the hamburger platter I was bringing him and said, "What did I do? What did I do?"

"You're putting too much chlorine in the pool," said the guest. "It hurt my eyes on that last dive."

"Sorry, sir," I said. "I won't let it happen again."

A little later, a fourteen-year-old daughter of one of our friends complained to Muriel that there were no

Popsicles in the refrigerator. Muriel nearly dropped the tray of drinks she was carrying, but she recovered sufficiently to hiss, through clenched teeth, "Why don't you go out and try to take one of Henry's bones away from him, dear?"

By the middle of July, I was exhausted and my work production had fallen off nearly to zero. Muriel had developed an allergy—constant runny nose, swollen and itchy eyes, occasional hives. Henry now had to sleep fourteen hours a day instead of his usual twelve, to rest up from his weekends. Even Steave and Janie, who helped us handle the mobs, were worn out.

After we had dispatched the last of the guests on a Sunday night, Steave said, "If you're goin' to run this place like a hotel, why don't you put in a desk and a room clerk and take reservations?" That thought, expressed in cynical jest, nevertheless started our reasoning processes working. Muriel and I discussed it and finally we hit on a plan.

First, I called Carol in and spoke sternly to her about the psychology course she had flunked in college the year before. "But why bring that up now, Daddy?" she said. "It didn't seem to bother you too much at the time, and besides, I've got another two years to make it up."

"No daughter of *mine* carries an F on her record," I bellowed. "It just so happens I found out you can go to the second summer-school session at the University of Connecticut and erase that shameful blot."

After tolerating the standard amount of weeping, I

softened the blow by pointing out that our state university has a couple of dozen beautiful tennis courts on which Carol could play during all the hours but the one a day she'd be in class. The weeping stopped and a few days later our daughter was packed off to school at Storrs, Connecticut, about eighty miles away. That eliminated one source of congestion at the house—the large, scholarly young men and the angular girls with long, dank hair.

The next step in our master plan was to phone everyone we knew and tell them we were going to California on writing assignments. We nearly blew this part of the plan because at least a half dozen people suggested that they would be glad to help us out by moving into the house and taking care of the pool and everything while we were away. The first time this happened, Muriel made a quick save by saying, "Oh, no, thank you very much, but Bill's mother and father are staying here until we get back," and this became her standard lie to the other Good Samaritans.

After all the calls were made, I installed a chain across the two gateposts of our driveway (a well-known local symbol that the owner of the house is not in residence), and I made sure that our car was in the garage at all times. We ventured out to do our marketing only after dark and I kept Henry in the back of the house so he could not be seen from the road. We invented a telephone code which we made known only to members of our family and close friends. If they wanted to reach us by phone, they had to wait for two rings, then hang up and immediately call again. We did not answer the phone otherwise. With all these precautions, we were able to enjoy a delightful two-week vacation in our own home. I regained my strength and my working patterns were restored. While Muriel's allergic reactions did not disappear, at least they seemed to be better.

The phone rang incessantly for the first week of our vacation and then the calls tapered off. By the end of the second week, we were only getting the two-ring code calls. We then decided it was safe for us to come out of hiding and we took down the chain, began to answer the phone normally, and resumed our natural existence.

We established a new procedure, however. We had gotten into trouble before because Muriel, in the first flush of her excitement over our spa, had bubblingly issued blanket invitations to all and sundry "to drop in any time." Now we used a strict reservation system, with no bubbling. We only had two guests at once and when we wanted to be alone, we discovered the best way to keep self-invitees away was for Muriel to fall back on the tried-and-true "Bill's mother and father are visiting us." In August, when my parents actually *did* spend a weekend with us, we had an almost impossible time convincing Steave and Janie that this really was the case. They thought we were using the gimmick against *them*. To preserve our relationship, we had to drop into the Bjelko house with my father and mother. Even so, Steave was skeptical for a time. He had picked up much of the facts and patois of show business from his close association with us, and he took me aside and said, "Are you sure they ain't actors from Central Casting?" I had my mother pull out an old pocket photo of me running hurdles for the NYU track team in 1939 (I could never figure out why she always carried this particular photo with her, but now I was grateful that she did) and Steave's Yankee suspicions subsided.

During this period of peaceful coexistence with our outside world, we had plenty of time for reflection and we began to realize that our house had strange effects on people. For example, an actor we know arrived for a two-day stay. Usually this man is one of the biggest hams in show business, doing a ten-minute act, as he puts it, "when the light goes on in the refrigerator." We dreaded taking him around with us on our daily chores —which he insisted on doing so he could "absorb all this wonderful Americana." I had been in shops with him in Hollywood where he had done such things as inserting photo flash bulbs in his nostrils and complaining about how his cold was killing him. "If he does that in Paul Carroccio's market I'll die," Muriel lamented.

Our guest was unusually subdued, however, even before we started out on our tour of the neighborhood. He called me aside and said, "You know, I really dig this New England atmosphere. It's what I used to dream about when I was a kid in Brooklyn. Do me a favor, will you? Don't tell anybody who I am. Use my maiden name. I'll wear these big dark glasses and if anybody says I look like me, kid around and say I'm always mistaken for me. I want to drink all this in and if anybody recognizes me they'll make a big fuss and I won't really get to see anything."

We took our guest to Earl Taylor's quaint village hardware shop and to Paul Carroccio's quaint village market and to Brian Burnell's quaint village pharmacy. We visited Dr. Tom Dwyer's office in his converted two-hundred-year-old crossroads blacksmith shop and we showed him the breathtaking forty-mile view of the Housatonic River valley from Jim Perkins' home on the bluff overlooking Candlewood Lake. We dropped in at the Old Schoolhouse antique shop, which actually is in an authentic Colonial old schoolhouse. No one recognized our friend—or, at least, no one dropped his traditional Yankee reserve to *let on* that he knew him—and the guest returned home tired and happy. "Great, *great*," he kept saying. "This is the first time I've really *lived* in years."

He was still saying, "Great, *great*," the next morning, when he made ready to leave in his Rolls-Royce. But the instant he got behind the wheel of the Rolls, his manner began to change. He kissed Muriel good-bye with absent-minded distraction and then he said to me, "Tell me honestly, Bill, could I be all washed up at the age of forty?"

"Of course not," I said. "What makes you say a thing like that?"

He muttered, "Not *one* person, not *one* person recognized me." And he drove off in a cloud of dust.

Perhaps the most common effect our house seemed to

have on our big-city guests was lethargy. For some reason we could never fathom, the most frenetic New York and Hollywood types would arrive, and after a swim in the pool, a game of ping-pong or a walk in the woods, complete and total collapse would set in. For example, one friend, a live-wire movie press agent named David Foster, came to the house on a Friday afternoon, fell asleep in a chair immediately after dinner, and was in bed by nine o'clock. He slept until noon the next day, had lunch and a swim and retired for an afternoon nap from three o'clock until six. He was in bed again for the night at 10 P.M. and repeated the same schedule on Sunday. When he left he apologized and yawned, "I guess it's the altitude." This puzzled us because our altitude was one thousand feet and he had just come from a movie premiere at mile-high Denver, where, he had assured us, he had been up swinging until three o'clock every morning.

It was the same with Jay Weston, a movie producer, and his wife, Hill. They made a big point about being 7 A.M. risers who just *had* to have coffee the moment they awakened. Since Muriel and I had no desire to be up that early on a weekend, I made an elaborate hookup of the electric coffeepot to a timing device that would cause it to commence perking at six-thirty. The sun was barely up when we heard the coffeepot bubbling and gurgling in the kitchen. Henry heard it, too, and mistakenly sensing an invasion of the premises, he began to growl. The combination of gurgling and growling finally became unbearable and Muriel and I got up and had some of the coffee ourselves. The Westons, who had bragged the night before that not one day in their lives had they slept beyond 7 A.M., did not arise from their slumber until it was nearly noon.

The natives, on the other hand, seemed to become restless on our premises. Steave, for one, was converted by our atmosphere into a practical joker—a proclivity he had never exhibited very much before. One day, for example, the phone rang and a voice said, "This is the Connecticut Highway Department. We got a complaint that your swimming pool is pouring out all over the road." I rushed outside and up to the pool and the fifteen thousand gallons of water all seemed to be still placidly in place. Then I looked up and Steave was walking over from his side of the mountain, head thrown back and bellowing with laughter. "I really *got* you with that phone call, didn't I?" he guffawed. Janie too, began to act strangely that summer. She conferred more and more frequently with Naomi on recipes, and one day she said to me, "I don't know anything about wines. Could you make up a list for me about what wine goes with what meat onto it and all?" The next thing we knew, she no longer was serving her wonderful New England boiled dinners and country-style spare ribs. Now, when we came over for dinner, it was Beef Stroganoff or Rock Cornish Game Hen Provençale, or some such.

Perhaps the most dramatic display of native restlessness came when we had a cocktail reception for some of my cronies in the local Democratic party. The affair started with the usual amount of Yankee reserve, but as the evening wore on, we went through eighteen bottles of booze and ordinarily restrained men and women were doing such things as hoisting me up on their shoulders and proclaiming me "the next State Senator from the 24th Senatorial District of the State of Connecticut."

At about 11 P.M., I realized I had neglected to feed Henry, who in his ardor at playing the role of co-host had himself completely forgotten about eating. I filled our beast's bowl with turkey leftovers, put it on the floor in the kitchen in its customary place, and I rejoined the merriment in the living room.

About five minutes later, Naomi came rushing in with a look of bewilderment on her face and she murmured to me, "Them folkses is eatin' Henry's dinner."

Muriel and I hastened into the kitchen, and there indeed were a lumber-company executive, a distinguished local attorney and a Town Committee chairman—all on the floor dining out of Henry's bowl, with Henry himself looking amiably on.

Muriel, who had had a particularly bad allergy attack that day, felt better for the first time and she laughed so hard that tears sprang from her smarting eyes. "At the Braeburn Inn," she said, "we set the finest table in Connecticut."

chapter xiv

As the summer drew to its close, Muriel's allergy problems became worse. We went to see doctors in both Connecticut and New York and they made tests and gave her pills but nothing really worked. Even Henry became an object of suspicion for a while and multiple tests were made on samples of his shaggy coat. The doctor who did that was our friend Tom Dwyer in New Fairfield. A few days after he made the tests, I went to see him in his office and I found him staring dreamily out the window. "How about Henry's coat?" I asked.

"Negative," he said, "but the damnedest thing happened yesterday. I left Henry's fur on the windowsill and a robin swooped down and swiped it and he used it to line his nest over in that tree over there. If *that* isn't the height of luxury." He was still muttering about the fur-lined nest as I left.

Another doctor suggested Muriel's allergy problem might be psychogenic in origin. "Watch for her reaction to stress," he told me. "If the nose and the eyes get worse after something upsetting happens, I think we've got the answer."

I then began to keep a log of the happenings that might affect Muriel's psyche. The pool began to leak and Vito told me it would cost me another five hundred dollars to fix it, the guarantee being no good because the pool company went out of business onto it and all. On hearing this distressing news, I wept but Muriel's allergy actually cleared up for a few days.

Then we were visited by a friend from Hollywood, a movie executive named David Golding. Golding was the most extreme case we had seen so far of the slumberitis that seemed to affect our out-of-town visitors. He fell asleep in a rocking chair and actually rocked back so far that the chair gently went over and Golding, in a more imaginative pratfall than any ever dreamed up by Mack Sennett, ended up continuing his slumbers with his feet in the air and the back of his bald head resting on the floor. Muriel roared with laughter for about a half hour and I quickly checked her allergic reaction. It was worse.

I reported these findings to the doctor. "Negative," he said, "but keep watching."

But suddenly there was nothing to watch for. All the symptoms mysteriously disappeared for a while.

"Maybe," said Muriel, "I'm allergic to allergy doctors."

chapter xv

O ne of the reasons we had wanted to live in the country was to escape the inexorable advance of automation. It was driving us crazy in the city. They had automated the elevators in our apartment building, for example, and suddenly we found ourselves living in a very expensive walkup. Our apartment was on the second floor, to which the computer minds of the elevators seemed to have taken an aversion and they rarely, if ever, stopped there. If both elevators were down in the lobby, just one floor below, they would stubbornly sit there paying no attention whatever to our frantic button-pushing, and then they would abruptly shoot up to the twenty-second floor.

Muriel had spent a lot of time studying the idiosyncrasies of our automated elevators, and one day she pointed out a pattern in their transistorized stupidity.

"Watch this," she said to me, and she pushed the down button on our second floor. One of the elevators, which had been resting at seven, immediately went into action and came to rest at the *third* floor. She pushed the button again. The other elevator came down from the penthouse, and it, too, stopped at the third floor. I danced around, singing, "She's got it! By George, she's got it!" I rushed down to the basement, on foot as usual, and reported Muriel's findings to Mr. Jacobsen, the superintendent. "Your elevators," I had proudly announced, "are programmed to stop at three when they're supposed to stop at two."

Jacobsen had then called in the elevator people and they worked on the monsters for a week. After they left, Muriel hastened out to test the new electronic programming. When she had returned to the apartment, I asked her, "How goes the battle of man over machine?"

"Great," she replied gloomily. "Now the blasted elevators stop at two all right, but they only go to one place—the basement."

And then there were the charge accounts. Every month, I'd receive dozens of automated bills with punched return-payment cards, warning me almost on pain of death not to "fold, staple or mutilate in any way." I got so nervous about anybody inadvertently folding my mail, thus probably adding $100,000 to a bill, that I sent Naomi down to await the postman every morning lest he crush and mutilate a return-payment card as he stuffed it into my mailbox.

The credit cards were the worst. Once I had to phone

Carte Blanche in California to protest a discrepancy in my account and they wouldn't talk to me when I simply used my name. I had to identify myself as 940-825-798-5, 640 E. 56th St., New York, N. Y., 10022, telephone number 212-753-6548, with bank account number 0210-0023-08-82-552.

I had developed a running feud with Carte Blanche because one day I had foolishly asked for a supplementary credit card for Muriel. I received a letter praising me for my foresight in making such a request, but the automated credit-card machine apparently never received a copy of the letter because Muriel's card didn't arrive. I wrote again, informing the machines that 940-825-798-5 was still supplementary-cardless, and I received a letter of regret about my having lost *my* card and notifying me that they were sending another one, with my name now becoming 940-737-652-7. I wrote back, reporting that 940-825-798-5 hadn't lost *his* card, that he had grown fond of 940-825-798-5, that he didn't think 940-737-652-7 suited him at all, and that he'd prefer to forget about the supplementary credit card for Mrs. 940-825-798-5. By return mail I received another expression of regret about having lost my *second* card and sternly informing me that they had changed my name *again* to 940-643-501-9 and to be more careful about this new number than I had been with my previous ones. I gave up then, but chose the most fiendish method of revenge I could think of. I had Henry bite two extra holes in my return-payment punch card.

When we moved to the country, we apparently had

left all this behind us. Muriel came to me one day and showed me a neat batch of what appeared to be handwritten notes.

"What are those?" I asked suspiciously. "Letters from your sister about her hair?"

"No," she said, "they're bills from our local charge accounts—nice, simple, old-fashioned, hand-written bills."

I said, "You mean we can fold, staple and mutilate them at will?"

"We sure can," she replied. And we spent the next hour in an orgy of bill mutilation.

We lived a pleasant computerless existence right up until the end of that second summer—the time of Muriel's allergy remission. We'd receive nice friendly bills from Gassner's Restaurant and the Henry Dick furniture store and such, and we'd exult in the fact that once again we were names, not numbers.

At the end of that August, however, we found out rudely that there was no escape. We received a letter from our Connecticut bank informing us joyously that automation had at last come to its Danbury branch and that they were delighted to inform us that thenceforth we would be known as 0211-0042-2562672245.

"Oh, *no!*" said Muriel with anguish.

"Well," I said philosophically, "at least we've got some status around here. That's a much bigger number than we had in any of our New York banks."

"0211-0042-2562672245," mused Muriel, letting the numbers run trippingly off her tongue. "In a way it *does* have a sort of melodic sound to it. Maybe we can get to love it after a while."

"Who knows?" I mused. "In a little town like this, maybe they have *little* computers with only *little* bad habits."

"Dreamer," said Muriel. "What would 0211-0042-2562672245 like to have for dinner tonight?"

The next day I went to our friendly little neighborhood bank to make a $2,500 deposit. The manager, an earnest young man named Bob, greeted me as usual with a cheery, "Hi, Bill."

"Don't get familiar," I said coolly. "From now on, *you* are 0211 and *I* am the eighteen-digit number you gave me. My friends here can call me 2245 for short. But let's not regress back to that old-fashioned name-calling business again."

0211 slapped his thigh and broke up with laughter. "Oh, you writer fellers," he chuckled. "Always coming up with a quip onto it and all."

"Yes," I said grimly.

About a week later I received my monthly statement from the bank. I gave it the usual cursory glance, just to make sure I wasn't on the verge of being overdrawn, and to my astonishment, I *was*. I ran my eye up the deposits column and the $2,500 deposit I had just made was not there. I rushed to the phone and called the bank. It being a very small branch, Bob, the manager, answered himself.

"0211," I said briskly, "this is 2245."

"*Who?*" he yelled.

"Davidson," I growled. "Bill Davidson."

"Oh, you writers," he giggled.

"Never mind that stuff," I said. "What happened to my $2,500 deposit? The next thing I know, you'll be bouncing my checks."

"As a matter of fact," he said, "I was just going to call you about that. We had to send thirteen of your checks back marked 'insufficient funds.'"

"You *what?*" I roared. "I just put $2,500 in the bank. I have the receipt right here. Why isn't that $2,500 on my statement?"

A note of panic crept into Bob's voice. "By God, you *did* deposit $2,500. That was the day you came in and called me by some funny number instead of my name. Let me check and get back to you."

Late that afternoon Bob phoned back. I could tell how worried he was just by the way he said hello. "We can't find it," he said.

"That's ridiculous," I said. "How could a $2,500 deposit just disappear?"

"I don't know," he said, sweating over the phone, "but it's got to be here *somewhere*. Anyway, we've stopped bouncing your checks."

"That's nice of you," I said, "but make sure to tell it to your computer."

"We'll keep in touch," he said.

"We sure will," I said.

The next day Bob called to inform me that he had looked behind all desks and in all crevices in the bank and the check was still missing. The following day he phoned to say he personally had been to the town dump and had gone through the bank's wastepaper-basket refuse for the entire week. "Can you imagine how lucky we are?" he said. "There's a strike on and they haven't burned it yet."

"That's pretty lucky," I said. "Do you have the check?"

"No," he said.

On the third day, Muriel and I went in person to see 0211 at the bank. We found him plunged in gloom. "This is more serious than you think," he said. "I just found out that if we don't find the check, *I'm* responsible for it—and that's almost a half a year's pay onto it and all."

"Why don't you dock the computer?" I suggested. The look of anguish he gave me made me sorry I said that. So did the kick I received from Muriel from behind the desk.

Just then one of 0211's girls came into his cubicle. "Mr. Richardson is on the phone from Texas," she said.

"Go away," said 0211.

"But he says it's about that little checking account he set up for his son who's at camp somewhere near here in the Berkshires," said the girl.

"Handle it yourself," said 0211, holding his head.

"But he insists on talking to *you*," persisted the girl. "He thinks his son is in trouble and he wants you to help him. He can't figure out how the boy only gets a twenty-dollar-a-week allowance and he makes a $2,500 deposit."

"What do I care if some damned kid—" began 0211. Then he executed a perfect double take and sprang upright in his chair. "Did you say $2,500?" he shouted.

"I've been trying to tell you onto it and all—" said the girl.

"Never mind," said 0211, "I'll talk to him. What did you say his name was? Davidson?"

"No, Richardson," said the girl, and she left.

0211 seized the phone and we could hear him say, "Of course, Mr. Richardson. . . . It was just a little mistake, Mr. Richardson. You see, it was posted to the wrong account. . . . Yes, sir, I'm glad you see it our way. . . . I hope this little error hasn't inconvenienced you. . . . No, the boy's all right. The biggest withdrawal we have for him is, let's see now, six dollars and seventy-five cents. . . . Yes, sir. . . . Yes, sir. . . . I understand your concern, sir, but these machines *do* take a little time to get shaken down, you know. . . . Ha! Ha! Ha! That's right. Frankenstein *did* have a little trouble with *his* machine, didn't he? . . . Oh, you Texans always coming up with a quip onto it and all. . . . Yes, sir. . . . Thank you, sir. . . . Good-bye, sir."

0211 hung up and slumped back in his chair.

"You've found it," said Muriel.

0211 nodded.

"Was it the automation?" I asked.

0211 nodded.

"How?" I asked.

0211 sighed. "Simple," he said. "you're 2245—at least your last four digits are. Richardson is 2235. The girl pushed the wrong button."

0211 was so shaken that we didn't have the heart to rub it in.

On the way out, however, I couldn't resist getting Henry out of the car, where he had been waiting, and I instructed him to relieve himself on the front window of the bank. Which he did.

As we drove away, Muriel remarked, "As my Welsh grandmother always used to say, 'Automation is the devil's plaything.'"

"How the hell could she say that?" I asked. "Your Welsh grandmother died nearly thirty years ago and we didn't even have the curse of automation then."

"My Welsh grandmother," said Muriel, "was wise beyond her years."

chapter xvi

Muriel's period of remission from her allergy ended about the time of our tussle with local automation, and after conferring with our psychogenic doctor, Tom Dwyer (a brilliant ex-New York City physician, who like ourselves was a refugee from the metropolis) ordered her to spend a week in the confines of our air-conditioned bedroom. "What does that mean?" I asked Tom.

He shrugged helplessly and said, "We want to see if maybe she's allergic to the pollens and all kinds of things we have in the air here in the country."

A chill went through me and for the first time I began to think of the possibility that we might have to sell our hard-won paradise and move back to the city. I said to Tom, "You mean all that soot and sulphur dioxide and carbon monoxide she breathes in the city is *healthier?"* Tom, a neo-rural philosopher, merely shrugged again.

Our fears were heightened when, after two days in the cooled and filtered air of the bedroom, the hives and the eye-and-nose swelling disappeared and Muriel's breathing became normal again—just as it always did after she had spent a couple of days in the city.

We had to wait out the rest of the week, however, so we settled down to reflect about the wonderful new world we had found and which we possibly were going to lose. We realized we loved it so because basically it was a kind world, a simple world. Even the unpleasant things—like prejudice—were of a less complex, more tractable, old-fashioned, turn-of-the-century nature. Generally, the Yankees disliked the Irish, the Irish disliked the Italians, the Italians disliked the Poles, the Poles disliked the Arabs, and so on down the line to the Negroes, who only recently had begun to demand equal rights.

And yet when election time came around, a remarkable ethnic amalgamation took place in both parties, not only in the choice of candidates, but also gastronomically. At various political functions, Muriel and I joined Irish-Americans happily eating clams with the Yankees; Italian-Americans munching *kibbee* with the Arabs; Portuguese-Americans nibbling *kielbasi* with the Poles, etc. With all the grumbling about the NAACP (most Danburians weren't even aware yet of the considerably more militant Negro-rights organizations such as CORE and SNCC), few people opposed public housing and other measures to better the lot of the underprivileged Negro resident, and Negro children frequently were elected to office in student organizations in the schools. The most distinguished citizen of the town was Marian Anderson, and her activities were proudly and consistently chronicled on page one of the Danbury *News-Times*. The area's favorite disk jockey was a Negro named Dick Alexander on radio station WINE, and in the many baby and beauty contests which Muriel and I habitually were asked to judge, Negroes were commonplace among the contestants.

The generally friendly, uncomplicated life of the community being what it was, I spent a good deal of my time on the telephone conversing with total strangers. I'd write a magazine article for one of the national magazines and Danburians and New Fairfielders would call up and discuss it with me on the phone. Frequently I got calls from our legislators, who would ask my advice on a bill before they introduced it in the State Senate or the General Assembly in Hartford. My own entry into politics came because I wrote an irate letter to the "Opinions of the People" column of the Danbury *News-Times* on the subject of highway safety, and the very next day I was phoned by two then-strangers, Jim Perkins and Chet Witters of the New Fairfield Democratic Town Committee. The following week they had me in Hartford, talking with Governor John Dempsey, in his office. A week later I was appointed to the local Safety Commission.

Even sin in our community had a simple, charming,

old-fashioned flavor to it. First of all, it was hard to find, which allayed Muriel's fears after all the books about exurbia she had read. When we first arrived, we heard all sorts of horrendous tales from Steave and Janie and others about extramarital escapades among the natives. Having both been Hollywood reporters, Muriel and I were equipped to evaluate such rumors and we soon found out that an alleged case of adultery was no more than a man becoming fog-bound and staying overnight in New Haven, or a woman having too much to drink at a party and sitting chastely on another man's lap.

One day, for example, Steave came over to the house and told a lurid story about an ex-movie star, now an occasional TV actress, who lived in the vicinity. "Poor woman, her husband running away with a nurse onto it and all," he declared. Steave is always a gentleman and a prurient detail has never passed his lips, but so graphic was his report of the husband-nurse affair that we totally believed it. A few weeks later, we ran into the actress in question at a movie-industry dinner in Hollywood, and there she sat, affectionately holding hands with her husband. We got involved in a long conversation with them about our mutual health and then Muriel, being feminine by nature, asked, "What happened to that nurse you used to have around your place?"

"Oh, you mean Emma?" said the actress pleasantly. "You know Emma was going with that doctor over in New Milford. Well, she finally snagged him and she ran off and got married when we left to come out here."

Another time, Steave, a Republican, found out that I was associating with Democrats like Jim Perkins and Chet Witters, and he took me aside confidentially and said, "It's none of my business onto it and all, kiddo, but that's a pretty wild crowd you're runnin' with. They have parties and at the end of the evenin' the husbands throw all their house keys onto the floor and all, and then the wives pick a key and they go home with the husband it belongs to." He added darkly, *"Not* their own."

We promptly forgot about this bit of gossip, but then, a few weeks later, we were invited to a party at the Witters house. Steave's admonition came back to Muriel at this point and she brooded all week about what she was going to do when the keys were thrown on the floor. I personally went out and spent eighteen dollars on a gold key—just to show how much class I had, and also so Muriel could readily identify it and grab it in the clutch. Otherwise she wouldn't go.

We went to the party and the punch and booze flowed freely and we had a wonderful time. The naughtiest things that happened were Joe Bates taking all the women's shoes off and putting them in the re-frigerator—a custom which he apparently had followed for years; and Chet Witters poking Muriel in the ribs every few minutes and making her stand up and sing the Fight Song of the University of Minnesota, which she had attended.

At about 2 A.M., the party began to break up and

husbands and wives made ready to depart. Noticing that they were leaving *together*, I said to Witters, "How about the keys?" He looked at me blankly. I said, "You know. In the middle of the floor onto it and all."

Realization dawned on Chet's face. "Oh, *that!*" he said. "We made up that story *ourselves* a couple of years ago. We were just trying to embarrass the Republicans about what a wild den of iniquity New Fairfield was getting to be under their administration."

No doubt there *was* sin in our particular section of rural Connecticut—what with the summer residents coming up from New York and human nature being what it is onto it and all—but the only times Muriel and I ran across it was strictly by accident. One night I got home late from a trip to Hartford and we wanted to go out for dinner, but we found that all of our favorite restaurants had already closed for the evening. We drove down Highway 37 and there on the left was Jim Barbarie's, neon signs ablaze. We went in and had an excellent steak dinner, and just as I had paid the check and we were making ready to leave, the waitress asked, "Aren't you going to stay for the show?"

"What show?" inquired Muriel.

"Why, we've got the best show in town here," said the waitress.

"What," asked Muriel, "is in the show?"

"An exotic dancer," replied the girl.

"And what," asked Muriel, "is an exotic dancer?" I knew but I didn't say anything.

"Oh," explained the waitress, "kind of Oriental and stuff like that."

We decided to wait and a few minutes later the show began. A three-piece musical combination played dispiritedly for a while, and then, with a fanfare of trumpet, the exotic dancer was introduced. She swept onto the floor and without wasting any time, she began to do enthusiastic bumps and grinds, using a chair as a prop. "That's not exotic; it's erotic," said Muriel.

"I know, dear," I said.

Suddenly, without pausing in her gyrations, the girl began to disrobe.

"Why, that's a strip tease," exclaimed Muriel, "and right here in quiet old Danbury."

"I know, dear," I said.

The girl continued with her routine and suddenly Muriel gasped. "Why, that's not a strip tease," she said. "She's *naked*."

"I know, dear," I said.

It was, indeed, the most thorough strip I had ever seen—even on Chicago's North Rush Street or New Orleans' Bourbon Street in the old days. When the show ended, we left and we passed our host, Jim Barbarie, a burly ex-policeman, talking to a uniformed cop. We heard Barbarie say, "But, Joe, I book these acts out of New York and I asked the agent for a belly dancer for our Arabic clientele, and—"

The next time we dined at Jim Barbarie's, the show consisted of a folk singer wearing a red beard and sneakers. But the exotica kept sneaking in on future weekends and you could always find out when it was going to be there by keeping your ears open at the gas station or barbershop.

Our most dramatic exposure to sin-in-the-country came in a totally unexpected and pleasantly genial way. One day at the market in New Fairfield, Muriel was puzzling over the selection of a head of lettuce when a man came over and with a friendly neighborly manner explained how you can tell the best lettuce from its outside leaves. Muriel looked at the head she was holding, poked inside and said, "You're right. This is the worst head of lettuce in the bunch."

"You can't win 'em all," said the man cheerily. And he moved away.

After that, we ran into the man frequently and learned that his name was Marty and that he lived alone, about a half mile up the road from us. He was a wellspring of information on many subjects, such as how best to arrange marigolds in a bowl, how to graft yellow and pink roses onto a red rose bush, etc. His favorite expression, whenever we told him we had done something wrong, was that cheery "You can't win 'em all." He was the acme of rural neighborliness at all times.

One day Marty slapped me on the back and said, "You know, you and I are really in the same business. I'm in the publishing game, too, you know."

"Where?" I asked.

"Oh, right here at my place. Got the printing press in my basement. Nothing big like what you do, but I help to mold public opinion, too. Come up and look my plant over any time, any time at all." Marty slapped me heartily on the back again and took off.

When he left, Muriel was starry-eyed. "Imagine that," she said. "A little press in his basement, turning out pamphlets just like Tom Paine in the Revolutionary War."

A few nights later, she induced me to drop by with her to see Marty, the gallant pamphleteer. We drove up the road and when we arrived at his house there was a police car with flashing roof light outside the stucco structure. When we recovered from the surprise of this, Muriel, incensed, muttered, "Cossacks, probably interfering with a gallant man's right of free expression." When we got out of our car, however, it wasn't a Cossack at all. It was our friendly neighborhood State Policeman, Oscar Lopes.

"What's up, Oscar?" I asked.

Oscar nodded toward the house. "Two Feds making a pinch," he said. "Postal inspectors. It's Marty."

"What's the rap?" I said, using the police vernacular I always affected with Oscar.

"Pornography," he said. "Old Marty's got enough stuff in there to take care of every stag party in the East. You always call me 'our friendly neighborhood State Policeman.' I guess you could say Old Marty's 'our friendly neighborhood pornographer.' "

Muriel, for a change, was too stunned to say anything. We just stood there and watched and Marty came out in a few minutes, walking between the two Federal agents. He saw us and bowed, with Old World charm, in Muriel's direction.

"Like I told you," he said, "you can't win 'em all."

chapter xvii

At the end of Muriel's one-week confinement in our air-conditioned bedroom, we drove over to see Tom Dwyer in his office in New Fairfield. It took us only ten minutes to get there, but by the time we arrived Muriel's snuffling already had begun again. Tom examined her and shook his head. "What do we do now?" I asked. Tom didn't answer. He just pulled out a brand-new issue of a medical journal and showed us an article by a Dr. Herman A. Heise of Milwaukee. Dr. Heise had made an eighteen-year study of pollen allergies and this article was considered the definitive work on the subject.

"A sufferer from hay fever and other pollen-caused allergies," wrote Dr. Heise, "would be well-advised to live in the city rather than the country, and above all should avoid open country where there is morning ground fog."

"We sure have plenty of *that* up on the mountain," Muriel interjected.

I read on: "Cities are usually warmer than the surrounding countryside, and the updrafts resulting from this warmth carry pollen aloft, where it tends to be trapped at cloud level. Cool air descends on the adjacent countryside and carries concentrations of pollen with it. The circulation pattern can favor concentrations of pollen in ground fog."

I looked up at Tom. "What this is trying to tell me," I said, "is that we should sell the house and move back to the city."

"The way Muriel seems to be affected by the pollen," said Tom," I just wouldn't know what else to advise."

We thanked Tom and drove back to the house in silence, except for the peculiar noises Muriel was making through her nose. To soften the impending blow, I tried desperately to think of some villain from whom our new move would deliver us, but all of the local people with whom we had dealt had been so kind and fair that I found it difficult to seek relief in a Mr. Blandings complex. The only one who had victimized us was Vito, the swimming-pool man, who had reneged on all his promises, but Vito came from a town some miles away and since we had been stupid enough to fall for the fly-by-night swimming-pool racket, after all we had read about it, it probably was our fault. Nevertheless I said, lamely, "Well, at least we won't have to be swindled by Vito any more." The remark had no effect whatever on our flagging spirits.

We got home and broke the news to Carol and Naomi, both of whom wept. Henry, not comprehending but seeing everyone else crying, became distraught, too. I called Jay Morrow, the real estate man, and explained the situation to him. He began to tell me about his aunt in Vermont who had the same trouble but I cut him off by saying, "That's nice, Jay, but just put the house on the market." That afternoon, a Saturday, he drove out and planted a For Sale sign on the front lawn.

The sign hadn't been up for five minutes when there was a screeching of brakes in the driveway and Steave came charging in. "What's *this?*" he said. He had ripped the sign out by the roots and was holding it in his huge hands.

"Well, it's a complicated story," I said, "but to make it short, Muriel's allergic to Connecticut—at least she's allergic to the weeds and stuff that grow around here." We didn't feel like talking much so Steave left after a while and I put the sign back on the lawn.

The next morning I was listlessly throwing a ball around with Henry up on the back lawn. Suddenly I heard a babble of voices coming from the direction of Steave's house. I walked over to the stone fence with Henry, and there, marching toward us over the gentle rise of the mountain, was a small army of neighbors, with Steave in the vanguard. He carried a hoe in his hand and his spray equipment was strapped to his back. Behind him came Aaron and Adam and long, lean Carl Fransen and Jim Perkins and Earl Taylor and members of the King Street Firehouse, and the Ladies' Auxiliary of the firehouse. The men carried hoes and spray guns; the women bore bags of sandwiches and Thermos jugs of coffee. "Well," said Steave cheerily, "you've always been interested in the Minute Men around here onto it and all. The Minute Men have arrived." He bowed graciously toward the Auxiliary. "And the Minute Ladies, too."

Before I could say anything, he began barking orders, like the sergeant he had been in the 63rd Division in World War II, and the men began to march out to various sectors of our wild and wooded acreage. The women set up their paraphernalia on our picnic table, and some of them grabbed hoes, too. By now, Muriel and Carol and Naomi had come out of the house. Muriel and Carol were stunned, as I was, but Naomi let out a joyous stream of Spanish, seized a hoe and scrambled off into the woods with the others. Henry, who had never had so much company, was out of his mind with glee.

Finally the shock wore off and I said to Steave, "What are you *doing?*"

He said, "Don't you worry about a thing. We're goin' to get rid of everything that grows around here that's makin' Muriel sick. It's the least a good neighbor can do."

"But, Steave," I pleaded. "It's not just the stuff around here that's doing it. It's the whole *countryside*. What you're doing is like trying to bail out the ocean with a pail."

Muriel, who was crying, nudged me and said, "No, Steave, you're right. Go ahead and do what you're planning to do. It's a wonderful idea. Thank you. Thank you. And God bless you."

"Don't you worry about a thing," said Steave. And he charged up into the woods to take command of his platoon.

The men worked all day, chopping, hoeing and spraying, while the women served them sandwiches and coffee, just as if they had been at a fire. By the end of the afternoon, the entire three acres looked like a park. The tangled underbrush, the weeds, the poison ivy were all gone. Muriel kept crying through her allergenic snuffles.

At sundown, I broke out the booze and we all had a convivial time and Aaron and a couple of the others went in for a swim. At about eight-thirty, the Minute Men and Ladies gathered up their hoes and spray guns and Thermos jugs, cheerily said good-bye, and straggled over the mountain to their initial marshaling area, Steave's house. As Steave left, out of the corner of my eye I could see him rip up the For Sale sign again and take it away with him.

A few moments after they all had gone, I heard a car pulling into the driveway. Henry and I went out to see who was there, and it was Dr. Tom Dwyer

He joined us up on the patio and I gave him a Scotch and water and he said, "I heard what happened today. It really broke me up."

"Us, too," said Muriel.

"Well," said Tom, "it may do some good. Who knows? Stranger things have happened in this crazy field of allergenics."

"I doubt it," I said.

"So do I," said Tom, "and that's why I took my day off to drive into New York today. I was talking to some doctors at my old hospital down there and they told me about a new experimental antihistamine they just got from a drug house in Switzerland. It sounds like it just might work in Muriel's case. When I heard about your other neighbors chopping and hoeing today, I figured the least I could do was to drive down to the hospital and get you these pills."

He pulled a vial out of his pocket and said to Muriel, "Take one every four hours and let's see what happens."

He finished his Scotch and rose to leave. "My lands, I better go now," he said. "Rita must just about have my supper ready."

I walked with him out to his car. "Just do me one favor," he said. "If this drug works, don't tell the neighbors about it. I'd like them to remember this day as theirs alone."

"You bet," I said. And Dr. Tom drove off into the gentle night.

chapter xviii

It was a year later. Janie gave a dinner party to cele-brate the anniversary of Muriel's deliverance from the pollens, and it was like a meeting of war vet-erans discussing a successful military campaign in which they all had participated.

It was a wonderful party. Janie had her house mag-nificently decorated with floral arrangements she had learned from Muriel, but on the fireplace mantel sat a clump of ragweed, set out like a captured enemy flag, in token of triumph. One of the high points of the eve-ning came when Steave made a little speech and Muriel went over to the ragweed and sniffed it, ritualistically. I held my breath, but there were no ill effects.

Before dinner we sat around discussing world poli-tics, the civil rights revolution and such. Local matters came into the conversation only when there was brief talk about my running for the legislature. Muriel and the ladies became engrossed in a conversation about Connecticut's teen-age drinking laws. Outside, there was a hint of rain and millions of crickets were rubbing their little legs together. My wife did not even hear them.

At dinner, Janie presided at the head of the table wearing a magnificent dress she had bought with Muriel the previous week during an expedition to Lord & Taylor in New York City. The table was softly illuminated with candlelight. The menu consisted of Eggs à la Russe, Paella Valenciana à la Naomi, a Belgian endive salad, and a fresh fruit compote with kirschwasser. The wine was an excellent Pouilly-Fuissé 1959.

At the end of the meal, Janie rose to propose a toast.

"To the Davidsons," she said. "They've only been here two years—and already they're just like *us*."

ABOUT THE AUTHOR

BILL DAVIDSON is a journalist who has had both side-splitting and hair-raising adventures in World War II, at the North Pole, in the big-city lairs of the Cosa Nostra and in the Golden Shambles of Hollywood. In *The Crickets All Look Alike* he recounts one of his most fascinating adventures, or rather one vast *mis*adventure, as his city-bred household invades and establishes a beachhead in rural Connecticut. Born in Jersey City, New Jersey, and educated at New York University, where he was an inter-collegiate track star and editor of the campus literary magazine, Davidson was one of the best-known wartime soldier-correspondents for *Yank,* then went on to become a winner of many journalism awards as a writer and editor for *Collier's* and *Look*. He now is Editor-at-large of *The Saturday Evening Post*. His wife, Muriel, is a successful free-lance magazine writer, and they work side by side at adjoining typewriters in the pine-panelled studio they now have added to their 1740 Colonial home. Their favorite hobbies, while relaxing between paragraphs, are competing with their Old English Sheepdog, Henry, in hurdle races over the New England stone walls, building ingenious fences around the corn patch to outwit the local raccoons, and sparring, with boxing gloves, at least one hour a day.